The Sense of Beauty

Being the outline of aesthetic theory

by George Santayana

Dover Publications, Inc., New York

This Dover edition, first published in 1955, is an
unabridged and unaltered republication of the work
first published by Charles Scribner's Sons in 1896.

Standard Book Number: 486-20238-0

Library of Congress Catalog Card Number: 55-14673

Manufactured in the United States of America
Dover Publications, Inc.
180 Varick Street
New York, N.Y. 10014

PREFACE

THIS little work contains the chief ideas gathered together for a course of lectures on the theory and history of æsthetics given at Harvard College from 1892 to 1895. The only originality I can claim is that which may result from the attempt to put together the scattered commonplaces of criticism into a system, under the inspiration of a naturalistic psychology. I have studied sincerity rather than novelty, and if any subject, as for instance the excellence of tragedy, is presented in a new light, the change consists only in the stricter application to a complex subject of the principles acknowledged to obtain in our simple judgments. My effort throughout has been to recall those fundamental æsthetic feelings the orderly extension of which yields sanity of judgment and distinction of taste.

The influences under which the book has been written are rather too general and pervasive to admit of specification; yet the student of philosophy will not fail to perceive how much I owe to writers, both living and dead, to whom no honour could be added by my acknowledgments. I have usually omitted any reference to them in foot-notes or in the text, in order that the air of controversy might be avoided, and the reader might be enabled to compare what is said more directly with the reality of his own experience.

G. S.

SEPTEMBER, 1896.

CONTENTS

vii

PART III. FORM

PART IV. EXPRESSION

The Sense of Beauty

INTRODUCTION

THE sense of beauty has a more important place in life than æsthetic theory has ever taken in philosophy. The plastic arts, with poetry and music, are the most conspicuous monuments of this human interest, because they appeal only to contemplation, and yet have attracted to their service, in all civilized ages, an amount of effort, genius, and honour, little inferior to that given to industry, war, or religion. The fine arts, however, where æsthetic feeling appears almost pure, are by no means the only sphere in which men show their susceptibility to beauty. In all products of human industry we notice the keenness with which the eye is attracted to the mere appearance of things: great sacrifices of time and labour are made to it in the most vulgar manufactures; nor does man select his dwelling, his clothes, or his companions without reference to their effect on his æsthetic senses. Of late we have even learned that the forms of many animals are due to the survival by sexual selection of the colours and forms most attractive to the eye. There must therefore be in our nature a very radical and wide-spread tendency to observe beauty, and to value it. No account of the principles of the mind can be at all adequate that passes over so conspicuous a faculty.

That æsthetic theory has received so little attention from the world is not due to the unimportance of the subject of which it treats, but rather to lack of an adequate motive for speculating upon it, and to the small success of the occasional efforts to deal with it. Absolute curiosity, and love of comprehension for its own sake, are not passions we have much leisure to indulge: they require not only freedom from affairs but, what is more rare, freedom from prepossessions and from the hatred of all ideas that do not make for the habitual goal of our thought.

Now, what has chiefly maintained such speculation as the world has seen has been either theological passion or practical use. All we find, for example, written about beauty may be

3

divided into two groups: that group of writings in which philosophers have interpreted æsthetic facts in the light of their metaphysical principles, and made of their theory of taste a corollary or footnote to their systems; and that group in which artists and critics have ventured into philosophic ground, by generalizing somewhat the maxims of the craft or the comments of the sensitive observer. A treatment of the subject at once direct and theoretic has been very rare: the problems of nature and morals have attracted the reasoners, and the description and creation of beauty have absorbed the artists; between the two reflection upon æsthetic experience has remained abortive or incoherent.

A circumstance that has also contributed to the absence or to the failure of æsthetic speculation is the subjectivity of the phenomenon with which it deals. Man has a prejudice against himself: anything which is a product of his mind seems to him to be unreal or comparatively insignificant. We are satisfied only when we fancy ourselves surrounded by objects and laws independent of our nature. The ancients long speculated about the constitution of the universe before they became aware of that mind which is the instrument of all speculation. The moderns, also, even within the field of psychology, have studied first the function of perception and the theory of knowledge, by which we seem to be informed about external things; they have in comparison neglected the exclusively subjective and human department of imagination and emotion. We have still to recognize in practice the truth that from these despised feelings of ours the great world of perception derives all its value, if not also its existence. Things are interesting because we care about them, and important because we need them. Had our perceptions no connexion with our pleasures, we should soon close our eyes on this world; if our intelligence were of no service to our passions, we should come to doubt, in the lazy freedom of reverie, whether two and two make four.

Yet so strong is the popular sense of the unworthiness and insignificance of things purely emotional, that those who have taken moral problems to heart and felt their dignity have often been led into attempts to discover some external right and beauty of which our moral and æsthetic feelings should be perceptions or discoveries, just as our intellectual activity is, in men's opinion, a perception or discovery of external fact. These philosophers seem to feel that unless moral and æsthetic judgments are expressions of objective truth, and not merely expressions of human nature, they stand condemned of hopeless triviality. A judgment is not trivial, however, because it rests on human feelings; on the contrary, triviality consists in abstraction from human interests; only those judgments and opinions are truly insignificant which wander beyond the reach of verification, and have no function in the ordering and enriching of life.

Both ethics and æsthetics have suffered much from the prejudice against the subjective. They have not suffered more because both have a subject-matter which is partly objective. Ethics deals with conduct as much as with emotion, and therefore considers the causes of events and their consequences as well as our judgments of their value. Æsthetics also is apt to include the history and philosophy of art, and to add much descriptive and critical matter to the theory of our susceptibility to beauty. A certain confusion is thereby introduced into these inquiries, but at the same time the discussion is enlivened by excursions into neighbouring provinces, perhaps more interesting to the general reader.

We may, however, distinguish three distinct elements of ethics and æsthetics, and three different ways of approaching the subject. The first is the exercise of the moral or æsthetic faculty itself, the actual pronouncing of judgment and giving of praise, blame, and precept. This is not a matter of science but of character, enthusiasm, niceness of perception, and fineness of emotion. It is æsthetic or moral activity, while ethics and æsthetics, as sciences, are intellectual activities, having that æsthetic or moral activity for their subject-matter.

The second method consists in the historical explanation of conduct or of art as a part of anthropology, and seeks to discover the conditions of various types of character, forms of polity, conceptions of justice, and schools of criticism and of art. Of this nature is a great deal of what has been written on æsthetics. The philosophy of art has often proved a more tempting subject than the psychology of taste, especially to minds which were not so much fascinated by beauty itself as by the curious problem of the artistic instinct in man and of the diversity of its manifestations in history.

The third method in ethics and æsthetics is psychological, as the other two are respectively didactic and historical. It deals with moral and æsthetic judgments as phenomena of mind and products of mental evolution. The problem here is to understand the origin and conditions of these feelings and their relation to the rest of our economy. Such an inquiry, if pursued successfully, would yield an understanding of the reason why we think anything right or beautiful, wrong or ugly; it would thus reveal the roots of conscience and taste in human nature and enable us to distinguish transitory preferences and ideals, which rest on peculiar conditions, from those which, springing from those elements of mind which all men share, are comparatively permanent and universal.

To this inquiry, as far as it concerns æsthetics, the following pages are devoted. No attempt will be made either to impose particular appreciations or to trace the history of art and criticism. The discussion will be limited to the nature and elements of our æsthetic judgments. It is a theoretical inquiry and has no directly hortatory quality. Yet insight into the basis of our preferences, if it could be gained, would not fail to have a good and purifying influence upon them. It would show us the futility of a dogmatism that would impose upon another man judgments and emotions for which the needed soil is lacking in his constitution and experience; and at the same time it would relieve us of any undue diffidence or excessive tolerance towards aberrations of taste, when we know what are the broader grounds of preference and the habits that make for greater and more diversified æsthetic enjoyment.

Therefore, although nothing has commonly been less attractive than treatises on beauty or less a guide to taste than disquisitions upon it, we may yet hope for some not merely theoretical gain from these studies. They have remained so often without practical influence because they have been pursued under unfavourable conditions. The writers have generally been audacious metaphysicians and somewhat incompetent critics; they have represented general and obscure principles, suggested by other parts of their philosophy, as the conditions of artistic excellence and the essence of beauty. But if the inquiry is kept close to the facts of feeling, we may hope that the resulting theory may have a clarifying effect on the experience on which it is based. That is, after all, the use of theory. If when a theory is bad it narrows our capacity for observation and makes all appreciation vicarious and formal, when it is good it reacts favourably upon our powers, guides the attention to what is really capable of affording entertainment, and increases, by force of new analogies, the range of our interests. Speculation is an evil if it imposes a foreign organization on our mental life; it is a good if it only brings to light, and makes more perfect by training, the organization already inherent in it.

We shall therefore study human sensibility itself and our actual feelings about beauty, and we shall look for no deeper, unconscious causes of our æsthetic consciousness. Such value as belongs to metaphysical derivations of the nature of the beautiful, comes to them not because they explain our primary feelings, which they cannot do, but because they express, and in fact constitute, some of our later appreciations. There is no explanation, for instance, in calling beauty an adumbration of divine attributes. Such a relation, if it were actual, would not help us at all to understand why the symbols of divinity pleased. But in certain moments of contemplation, when much emotional experience lies behind us, and we have reached very general ideas both of nature and of life, our delight in any particular object may consist in nothing but the thought that this object is a manifestation of universal principles. The blue sky may come to please chiefly because it seems the image of a serene conscience, or of the eternal youth and purity of nature after a thousand partial corruptions. But this expressiveness of the sky is due to certain qualities of the sensation, which bind it to all things happy and pure, and, in a mind in which the essence of purity and happiness is embodied in an idea of God, bind it also to that idea.

So it may happen that the most arbitrary and unreal theories, which must be rejected as general explanations of æsthetic life, may be reinstated as particular moments of it. Those intuitions which we call Platonic are seldom scientific, they seldom explain the phenomena or hit upon the actual law of things, but they are often the highest expression of that activity which they fail to make comprehensible. The adoring lover cannot understand the natural history of love; for he is all in all at the last and supreme stage of its development. Hence the world has always been puzzled in its judgment of the Platonists; their theories are so extravagant, yet their wisdom seems so great. Platonism is a very refined and beautiful expression of our natural instincts, it embodies conscience and utters our inmost hopes. Platonic philosophers have therefore a natural authority, as standing on heights to which the vulgar cannot attain, but to which they naturally and half-consciously aspire.

When a man tells you that beauty is the manifestation of God to the senses, you wish you might understand him, you grope for a deep truth in his obscurity, you honour him for his elevation of mind, and your respect may even induce you to assent to what he says as to an intelligible proposition. Your thought may in consequence be dominated ever after by a verbal dogma, around which all your sympathies and antipathies will quickly gather, and the less you have penetrated the original sense of your creed, the more absolutely will you believe it. You will have followed Mephistopheles' advice:—

> Im ganzen haltet euch am Worte,
> So geht euch durch die sichere Pforte
> Zum Tempel der Gewissheit ein.

Yet reflection might have shown you that the word of the master held no objective account of the nature and origin of beauty, but was the vague expression of his highly complex emotions.

It is one of the attributes of God, one of the perfections which we contemplate in our idea of him, that there is no duality or opposition between his will and his vision, between the impulses of his nature and the events of his life. This is what we commonly designate as omnipotence and creation. Now, in the contemplation of beauty, our faculties of perception have the same perfection: it is indeed from the experience of beauty and happiness, from the occasional harmony between our nature and our environment, that we draw our conception of the divine life. There is, then, a real propriety in calling beauty a manifestation of God to the senses, since, in the region of sense, the perception of beauty exemplifies the adequacy and perfection which in general we objectify in an idea of God.

But the minds that dwell in the atmosphere of these analogies are hardly those that will care to ask what are the conditions and the varieties of this perfection of function, in other words, how it comes about that we perceive beauty at all, or have any inkling of divinity. Only the other philosophers, those that wallow in Epicurus' sty, know anything about the latter question. But it is easier to be impressed than to be instructed, and the public is very ready to believe that where there is noble language not without obscurity there must be profound knowledge. We should distinguish, however, the two distinct demands in the case. One is for comprehension; we look for the theory of a human function which must cover all possible cases of its exercise, whether noble or base. This the Platonists utterly fail to give us. The other demand is for inspiration; we wish to be nourished by the maxims and confessions of an exalted mind, in whom the æsthetic function is pre-eminent. By responding to this demand the same thinkers may win our admiration.

To feel beauty is a better thing than to understand how we

come to feel it. To have imagination and taste, to love the best, to be carried by the contemplation of nature to a vivid faith in the ideal, all this is more, a great deal more, than any science can hope to be. The poets and philosophers who express this æsthetic experience and stimulate the same function in us by their example, do a greater service to mankind and deserve higher honour than the discoverers of historical truth. Reflection is indeed a part of life, but the last part. Its specific value consists in the satisfaction of curiosity, in the smoothing out and explanation of things: but the greatest pleasure which we actually get from reflection is borrowed from the experience on which we reflect. We do not often indulge in retrospect for the sake of a scientific knowledge of human life, but rather to revive the memories of what once was dear. And I should have little hope of interesting the reader in the present analyses, did I not rely on the attractions of a subject associated with so many of his pleasures.

But the recognition of the superiority of æsthetics in experience to æsthetics in theory ought not to make us accept as an explanation of æsthetic feeling what is in truth only an expression of it. When Plato tells us of the eternal ideas in conformity to which all excellence consists, he is making himself the spokesman of the moral consciousness. Our conscience and taste establish these ideals; to make a judgment is virtually to establish an ideal, and all ideals are absolute and eternal for the judgment that involves them, because in finding and declaring a thing good or beautiful, our sentence is categorical, and the standard evoked by our judgment is for that case intrinsic and ultimate. But at the next moment, when the mind is on another footing, a new ideal is evoked, no less absolute for the present judgment than the old ideal was for the previous one. If we are then expressing our feeling and confessing what happens to us when we judge, we shall be quite right in saying that we have always an absolute ideal before us, and that value lies in conformity with that ideal. So, also, if we try to define that ideal, we shall hardly be able to say of it anything less noble and more definite than that it is the embodiment of an infinite good. For it is that incommunicable and illusive excellence that haunts every beautiful thing, and

like a star
Beacons from the abode where the eternal are.

For the expression of this experience we should go to the poets, to the more inspired critics, and best of all to the immortal parables of Plato. But if what we desire is to increase our knowledge rather than to cultivate our sensibility, we should do well to close all those delightful books; for we shall not find any instruction there upon the questions which most press upon us; namely, how an ideal is formed in the mind, how a given object is compared with it, what is the common element in all beautiful things, and what the substance of the absolute ideal in which all ideals tend to be lost; and, finally, how we come to be sensitive to beauty at all, or to value it. These questions must be capable of answers, if any science of human nature is really possible.—So far, then, are we from ignoring the insight of the Platonists, that we hope to explain it, and in a sense to justify it, by showing that it is the natural and sometimes the supreme expression of the common principles of our nature.

PART I

THE NATURE OF BEAUTY

§ 1. THE PHILOSOPHY OF BEAUTY IS A THEORY OF VALUES. It would be easy to find a definition of beauty that should give in a few words a telling paraphrase of the word. We know on excellent authority that beauty is truth, that it is the expression of the ideal, the symbol of divine perfection, and the sensible manifestation of the good. A litany of these titles of honour might easily be compiled, and repeated in praise of our divinity. Such phrases stimulate thought and give us a momentary pleasure, but they hardly bring any permanent enlightenment. A definition that should really define must be nothing less than the exposition of the origin, place, and elements of beauty as an object of human experience. We must learn from it, as far as possible, why, when, and how beauty appears, what conditions an object must fulfil to be beautiful, what elements of our nature make us sensible of beauty, and what the relation is between the constitution of the object and the excitement of our susceptibility. Nothing less will really define beauty or make us understand what aesthetic appreciation is. The definition of beauty in this sense will be the task of this whole book, a task that can be only very imperfectly accomplished within its limits.

The historical titles of our subject may give us a hint towards the beginning of such a definition. Many writers of the last century called the philosophy of beauty *Criticism,* and the word is still retained as the title for the reasoned appreciation of works of art. We could hardly speak, however, of delight in nature as criticism. A sunset is not criticised; it is felt and enjoyed. The word "criticism," used on such an occasion, would emphasize too much the element of deliberate judgment and of comparison with standards. Beauty, although often so described, is seldom so perceived, and all the greatest excellences of nature and art are so far from being approved of by a rule that they themselves furnish the standard and ideal by which critics measure inferior effects.

11

This age of science and of nomenclature has accordingly adopted a more learned word, *Æsthetics,* that is, the theory of perception or of susceptibility. If criticism is too narrow a word, pointing exclusively to our more artificial judgments, æsthetics seems to be too broad and to include within its sphere all pleasures and pains, if not all perceptions whatsoever. Kant used it, as we know, for his theory of time and space as forms of all perception; and it has at times been narrowed into an equivalent for the philosophy of art.

If we combine, however, the etymological meaning of criticism with that of æsthetics, we shall unite two essential qualities of the theory of beauty. Criticism implies judgment, and æsthetics perception. To get the common ground, that of perceptions which are critical, or judgments which are perceptions, we must widen our notion of deliberate criticism so as to include those judgments of value which are instinctive and immediate, that is, to include pleasures and pains; and at the same time we must narrow our notion of æsthetics so as to exclude all perceptions which are not appreciations, which do not find a value in their objects. We thus reach the sphere of critical or appreciative perception, which is, roughly speaking, what we mean to deal with. And retaining the word "æsthetics," which is not current, we may therefore say that æsthetics is concerned with the perception of values. The meaning and conditions of value is, then, what we must first consider.

Since the days of Descartes it has been a conception familiar to philosophers that every visible event in nature might be explained by previous visible events, and that all the motions, for instance, of the tongue in speech, or of the hand in painting, might have merely physical causes. If consciousness is thus accessory to life and not essential to it, the race of man might have existed upon the earth and acquired all the arts necessary for its subsistence without possessing a single sensation, idea, or emotion. Natural selection might have secured the survival of those automata which made useful reactions upon their environment. An instinct of self-preservation would have been developed, dangers would have been shunned without being feared, and injuries revenged without being felt.

In such a world there might have come to be the most perfect organization. There would have been what we should call the expression of the deepest interests and the apparent pursuit of conceived goods. For there would have been spontaneous and ingrained tendencies to avoid certain contingencies and to produce others; all the dumb show and evidence of thinking would have been patent to the observer. Yet there would surely have been no thinking, no expectation, and no conscious achievement in the whole process.

The onlooker might have feigned ends and objects of forethought, as we do in the case of the water that seeks its own level, or in that of the vacuum which nature abhors. But the particles of matter would have remained unconscious of their collocation, and all nature would have been insensible of their changing arrangement. We only, the possible spectators of that process, by virtue of our own interests and habits, could see any progress or culmination in it. We should see culmination where the result attained satisfied our practical or æsthetic demands, and progress wherever such a satisfaction was approached. But apart from ourselves, and our human bias, we can see in such a mechanical world no element of value whatever. In removing consciousness, we have removed the possibility of worth.

But it is not only in the absence of all consciousness that value would be removed from the world; by a less violent abstraction from the totality of human experience, we might conceive beings of a purely intellectual cast, minds in which the transformations of nature were mirrored without any emotion. Every event would then be noted, its relations would be observed, its recurrence might even be expected; but all this would happen without a shadow of desire, of pleasure, or of regret. No event would be repulsive, no situation terrible. We might, in a word, have a world of idea without a world of will. In this case, as completely as if consciousness were absent altogether, all value and excellence would be gone. So that for the existence of good in any form it is not merely consciousness but emotional consciousness that is needed. Observation will not do, appreciation is required.

§ 2. PREFERENCE IS ULTIMATELY IRRATIONAL. We may therefore at once assert this axiom, important for all moral philosophy and fatal to certain stubborn incoherences of thought, that there is no value apart from some appreciation of it, and no good apart from some preference of it before its absence or its opposite. In appreciation, in preference, lies the root and essence of all excellence. Or, as Spinoza clearly expresses it, we desire nothing because it is good, but it is good only because we desire it.

It is true that in the absence of an instinctive reaction we can still apply these epithets by an appeal to usage. We may agree that an action is bad, or a building good, because we recognize in them a character which we have learned to designate by that adjective; but unless there is in us some trace of passionate reprobation or of sensible delight, there is no moral or æsthetic judgment. It is all a question of propriety of speech, and of the empty titles of things. The verbal and mechanical proposition, that passes for judgment of worth, is the great cloak of ineptitude in these matters. Insensibility is very quick in the conventional use of words. If we appealed more often to actual feeling, our judgments would be more diverse, but they would be more legitimate and instructive. Verbal judgments are often useful instruments of thought, but it is not by them that worth can ultimately be determined.

Values spring from the immediate and inexplicable reaction of vital impulse, and from the irrational part of our nature. The rational part is by its essence relative; it leads us from data to conclusions, or from parts to wholes; it never furnishes the data with which it works. If any preference or precept were declared to be ultimate and primitive, it would thereby be declared to be irrational, since mediation, inference, and synthesis are the essence of rationality. The ideal of rationality is itself as arbitrary, as much dependent on the needs of a finite organization, as any other ideal. Only as ultimately securing tranquillity of mind, which the philosopher instinctively pursues, has it for him any necessity. In spite of the verbal propriety of saying that reason demands rationality, what really demands rationality, what makes it a good and indispensable thing and gives it all its authority, is not its own nature, but our need of it both in safe and economical action and in the pleasures of comprehension.

It is evident that beauty is a species of value, and what we have said of value in general applies to this particular kind. A first approach to a definition of beauty has therefore been made by the exclusion of all intellectual judgments, all judgments of matter of fact or of relation. To substitute judgments of fact for judgments of value, is a sign of a pedantic and borrowed criticism. If we approach a work of art or nature scientifically, for the sake of its historical connexions or proper classification, we do not approach it æsthetically. The discovery of its date or of its author may be otherwise interesting; it only remotely affects our æsthetic appreciation by adding to the direct effect certain associations. If the direct effect were absent, and the object in itself uninteresting, the circumstances would be immaterial.

Molière's *Misanthrope* says to the court poet who commends his sonnet as written in a quarter of an hour,

> Voyons, monsieur, le temps ne fait rien à l'affaire,

and so we might say to the critic that sinks into the archæologist, show us the work, and let the date alone.

In an opposite direction the same substitution of facts for values makes its appearance, whenever the reproduction of fact is made the sole standard of artistic excellence. Many half-trained observers condemn the work of some naïve or fanciful masters with a sneer, because, as they truly say, it is out of drawing. The implication is that to be correctly copied from a model is the prerequisite of all beauty. Correctness is, indeed, an element of effect and one which, in respect to familiar objects, is almost indispensable, because its absence would cause a disappointment and dissatisfaction incompatible with enjoyment. We learn to value truth more and more as our love and knowledge of nature increase. But fidelity is a merit only because it is in this way a factor in our pleasure. It stands on a level with all other ingredients of effect. When a man raises it to a solitary pre-eminence and becomes incapable of appreciating anything else, he betrays the decay of æsthetic capacity. The scientific habit in him inhibits the artistic.

That facts have a value of their own, at once complicates and explains this question. We are naturally pleased by every perception, and recognition and surprise are particularly acute sensations. When we see a striking truth in any imitation, we are therefore delighted, and this kind of pleasure is very legitimate, and enters into the best effects of all the representative arts. Truth and realism are therefore æsthetically good, but they are not all-sufficient, since the representation of everything is not equally pleasing and effective. The fact that resemblance is a source of satisfaction, justifies the critic in demanding it, while the æsthetic insufficiency of such veracity shows the different value of truth in science and in art. Science is the response to the demand for information, and in it we ask for the whole truth and nothing but the truth. Art is the response to the demand for entertainment, for the stimulation of our senses and imagination, and truth enters into it only as it subserves these ends.

Even the scientific value of truth is not, however, ultimate or absolute. It rests partly on practical, partly on æsthetic interests. As our ideas are gradually brought into conformity with the facts by the painful process of selection,—for intuition runs equally into truth and into error, and can settle nothing if not controlled by experience,—we gain vastly in our command over our environment. This is the fundamental value of natural science, and the fruit it is yielding in our day. We have no better vision of nature and life than some of our predecessors, but we have greater material resources. To know the truth about the composition and history of things is good for this reason. It is also good because of the enlarged horizon it gives us, because the spectacle of nature is a marvellous and fascinating one, full of a serious sadness and large peace, which gives us back our birthright as children of the planet and naturalizes us upon the earth. This is the poetic value of the scientific *Weltanschauung*. From these two benefits, the practical and the imaginative, all the value of truth is derived.

Æsthetic and moral judgments are accordingly to be classed together in contrast to judgments intellectual; they are both judgments of value, while intellectual judgments are judgments of fact. If the latter have any value, it is only derivative, and our whole intellectual life has its only justification in its connexion with our pleasures and pains.

§ 3. CONTRAST BETWEEN MORAL AND ÆSTHETIC VALUES. The relation between æsthetic and moral judgments, between the spheres of the beautiful and the good, is close, but the distinction between them is important. One factor of this distinction is that while æsthetic judgments are mainly positive, that is, perceptions of good, moral judgments are mainly and fundamentally negative, or perceptions of evil. Another factor of the distinction is that whereas, in the perception of beauty, our judgment is necessarily intrinsic and based on the character of the immediate experience, and never consciously on the idea of an eventual utility in the object, judgments about moral worth, on the contrary, are always based, when they are positive, upon the consciousness of benefits probably involved. Both these distinctions need some elucidation.

Hedonistic ethics have always had to struggle against the moral sense of mankind. Earnest minds, that feel the weight and dignity of life, rebel against the assertion that the aim of right conduct is enjoyment. Pleasure usually appears to them as a temptation, and they sometimes go so far as to make avoidance of it a virtue. The truth is that morality is not mainly concerned with the attainment of pleasure; it is rather concerned, in all its deeper and more authoritative maxims, with the prevention of suffering. There is something artificial in the deliberate pursuit of pleasure; there is something absurd in the obligation to enjoy oneself. We feel no duty in that direction; we take to enjoyment naturally enough after the work of life is done, and the freedom and spontaneity of our pleasures is what is most essential to them.

The sad business of life is rather to escape certain dreadful evils to which our nature exposes us,—death, hunger, disease, weariness, isolation, and contempt. By the awful authority of these things, which stand like spectres behind every moral injunction, conscience in reality speaks, and a mind which they have duly impressed cannot but feel, by contrast, the hopeless triviality of the search for pleasure. It cannot but feel that a life abandoned to amusement and to changing impulses must run unawares into fatal dangers. The moment, however, that society emerges from the early pressure of the environment and is tolerably secure against primary evils, morality grows lax. The forms that life will farther assume are not to be imposed by moral authority, but are determined by the genius of the race, the opportunities of the moment, and the tastes and resources of individual minds. The reign of duty gives place to the reign of freedom, and the law and the covenant to the dispensation of grace.

The appreciation of beauty and its embodiment in the arts are activities which belong to our holiday life, when we are redeemed for the moment from the shadow of evil and the slavery to fear, and are following the bent of our nature where it chooses to lead us. The values, then, with which we here deal are positive; they were negative in the sphere of morality. The ugly is hardly an exception, because it is not the cause of any real pain. In itself it is rather a source of amusement. If its suggestions are vitally repulsive, its presence becomes a real evil towards which we assume a practical and moral attitude. And, correspondingly, the pleasant is never, as we have seen, the object of a truly moral injunction.

§ 4. WORK AND PLAY. We have here, then, an important element of the distinction between æsthetic and moral values. It is the same that has been pointed to in the famous contrast between work and play. These terms may be used in different senses and their importance in moral classification differs with the meaning attached to them. We may call everything play

which is useless activity, exercise that springs from the physiological impulse to discharge the energy which the exigencies of
life have not called out. Work will then be all action that is
necessary or useful for life. Evidently if work and play are thus
objectively distinguished as useful and useless action, work is a
eulogistic term and play a disparaging one. It would be better
for us that all our energy should be turned to account, that none
of it should be wasted in aimless motion. Play, in this sense, is
a sign of imperfect adaptation. It is proper to childhood, when
the body and mind are not yet fit to cope with the environment,
but it is unseemly in manhood and pitiable in old age, because
it marks an atrophy of human nature, and a failure to take hold
of the opportunities of life.

Play is thus essentially frivolous. Some persons, understanding
the term in this sense, have felt an aversion, which every liberal
mind will share, to classing social pleasures, art, and religion
under the head of play, and by that epithet condemning them,
as a certain school seems to do, to gradual extinction as the race
approaches maturity. But if all the useless ornaments of our life
are to be cut off in the process of adaptation, evolution would
impoverish instead of enriching our nature. Perhaps that is the
tendency of evolution, and our barbarous ancestors amid their
toils and wars, with their flaming passions and mythologies,
lived better lives than are reserved to our well-adapted descend-
ants.

We may be allowed to hope, however, that some imagination
may survive parasitically even in the most serviceable brain.
Whatever course history may take,—and we are not here concerned with prophecy,—the question of what is desirable is not
affected. To condemn spontaneous and delightful occupations
because they are useless for self-preservation shows an uncritical
prizing of life irrespective of its content. For such a system the
worthiest function of the universe should be to establish perpetual motion. Uselessness is a fatal accusation to bring against
any act which is done for its presumed utility, but those which
are done for their own sake are their own justification.

At the same time there is an undeniable propriety in calling
all the liberal and imaginative activities of man play, because
they are spontaneous, and not carried on under pressure of external necessity or danger. Their utility for self-preservation may
be very indirect and accidental, but they are not worthless for
that reason. On the contrary, we may measure the degree of
happiness and civilization which any race has attained by the

proportion of its energy which is devoted to free and generous pursuits, to the adornment of life and the culture of the imagination. For it is in the spontaneous play of his faculties that man finds himself and his happiness. Slavery is the most degrading condition of which he is capable, and he is as often a slave to the niggardness of the earth and the inclemency of heaven, as to a master or an institution. He is a slave when all his energy is spent in avoiding suffering and death, when all his action is imposed from without, and no breath or strength is left him for free enjoyment.

Work and play here take on a different meaning, and become equivalent to servitude and freedom. The change consists in the subjective point of view from which the distinction is now made. We no longer mean by work all that is done usefully, but only what is done unwillingly and by the spur of necessity. By play we are designating, no longer what is done fruitlessly, but whatever is done spontaneously and for its own sake, whether it have or not an ulterior utility. Play, in this sense, may be our most useful occupation. So far would a gradual adaptation to the environment be from making this play obsolete, that it would tend to abolish work, and to make play universal. For with the elimination of all the conflicts and errors of instinct, the race would do spontaneously whatever conduced to its welfare and we should live safely and prosperously without external stimulus or restraint.

§ 5. ALL VALUES ARE IN ONE SENSE ÆSTHETIC. In this second and subjective sense, then, work is the disparaging term and play the eulogistic one. All who feel the dignity and importance of the things of the imagination, need not hesitate to adopt the classification which designates them as play. We point out thereby, not that they have no value, but that their value is intrinsic, that in them is one of the sources of all worth. Evidently all values must be ultimately intrinsic. The useful is good because of the excellence of its consequences; but these must somewhere cease to be merely useful in their turn, or only excellent as means; somewhere we must reach the good that is good in itself and for its own sake, else the whole process is futile, and the utility of our first object illusory. We here reach the second factor in our distinction, between æsthetic and moral values, which regards their immediacy.

If we attempt to remove from life all its evils, as the popular imagination has done at times, we shall find little but æsthetic pleasures remaining to constitute unalloyed happiness. The satisfaction of the passions and the appetites, in which we chiefly place earthly happiness, themselves take on an æsthetic tinge when we remove ideally the possibility of loss or variation. What could the Olympians honour in one another or the seraphim worship in God except the embodiment of eternal attributes, of essences which, like beauty, make us happy only in contemplation? The glory of heaven could not be otherwise symbolized than by light and music. Even the knowledge of truth, which the most sober theologians made the essence of the beatific vision, is an æsthetic delight; for when the truth has no further practical utility, it becomes a landscape. The delight of it is imaginative and the value of it æsthetic.

This reduction of all values to immediate appreciations, to sensuous or vital activities, is so inevitable that it has struck even the minds most courageously rationalistic. Only for them, instead of leading to the liberation of æsthetic goods from practical entanglements and their establishment as the only pure and positive values in life, this analysis has led rather to the denial of all pure and positive goods altogether. Such thinkers naturally assume that moral values are intrinsic and supreme; and since these moral values would not arise but for the existence or imminence of physical evils, they embrace the paradox that without evil no good whatever is conceivable.

The harsh requirements of apologetics have no doubt helped them to this position, from which one breath of spring or the sight of one well-begotten creature should be enough to dislodge them. Their ethical temper and the fetters of their imagination forbid them to reconsider their original assumption and to conceive that morality is a means and not an end; that it is the price of human non-adaptation, and the consequence of the original sin of unfitness. It is the compression of human conduct within the narrow limits of the safe and possible. Remove danger, remove pain, remove the occasion of pity, and the need of morality is gone. To say "thou shalt not" would then be an impertinence.

But this elimination of precept would not be a cessation of life. The senses would still be open, the instincts would still operate, and lead all creatures to the haunts and occupations that befitted them. The variety of nature and the infinity of art, with the companionship of our fellows, would fill the leisure of that ideal existence. These are the elements of our positive happiness, the things which, amid a thousand vexations and vanities, make the clear profit of living.

§ 6. ÆSTHETIC CONSECRATION OF GENERAL PRINCIPLES. Not only are the various satisfactions which morals are meant to secure æsthetic in the last analysis, but when the conscience is formed, and right principles acquire an immediate authority, our attitude to these principles becomes æsthetic also. Honour, truthfulness, and cleanliness are obvious examples. When the absence of these virtues causes an instinctive disgust, as it does in well-bred people, the reaction is essentially æsthetic, because it is not based on reflection and benevolence, but on constitutional sensitiveness. This æsthetic sensitiveness is, however, properly enough called moral, because it is the effect of conscientious training and is more powerful for good in society than laborious virtue, because it is much more constant and catching. It is καλοκἀγαθία, the æsthetic demand for the morally good, and perhaps the finest flower of human nature.

But this tendency of representative principles to become independent powers and acquire intrinsic value is sometimes mischievous. It is the foundation of the conflicts between sentiment and justice, between intuitive and utilitarian morals. Every human reform is the reassertion of the primary interests of man against the authority of general principles which have ceased to represent those interests fairly, but which still obtain the idolatrous veneration of mankind. Nor are chivalry and religion alone liable to fall into this moral superstition. It arises wherever an abstract good is substituted for its concrete equivalent. The miser's fallacy is the typical case, and something very like it is the ethical principle of half our respectable population. To the exercise of certain useful habits men come to sacrifice the advantage which was the original basis and justification of those habits. Minute knowledge is pursued at the expense of largeness of mind, and riches at the expense of comfort and freedom.

This error is all the more specious when the derived aim has in itself some æsthetic charm, such as belongs to the Stoic idea of playing one's part in a vast drama of things, irrespective of any advantage thereby accruing to any one; somewhat as the miser's passion is rendered a little normal when his eye is fascinated not merely by the figures of a bank account, but by the glitter of the yellow gold. And the vanity of playing a tragic part and the glory of conscious self-sacrifice have the same immediate fascination. Many irrational maxims thus acquire a kind of nobility. An object is chosen as the highest good which has not only a certain representative value, but also an intrinsic one,—which is not merely a method for the realization of other values, but a value in its own realization.

Obedience to God is for the Christian, as conformity to the laws of nature or reason is for the Stoic, an attitude which has a certain emotional and passionate worth, apart from its original justification by maxims of utility. This emotional and passionate force is the essence of fanaticism, it makes imperatives categorical, and gives them absolute sway over the conscience in spite of their one-sidedness and their injustice to the manifold demands of human nature.

Obedience to God or reason can originally recommend itself to a man only as the surest and ultimately least painful way of balancing his aims and synthesizing his desires. So necessary is this sanction even to the most impetuous natures, that no martyr would go to the stake if he did not believe that the powers of nature, in the day of judgment, would be on his side. But the human mind is a turbulent commonwealth, and the laws that make for the greatest good cannot be established in it without some partial sacrifice, without the suppression of many particular impulses. Hence the voice of reason or the command of God, which makes for the maximum ultimate satisfaction, finds itself opposed by sundry scattered and refractory forces, which are henceforth denominated bad. The unreflective conscience, forgetting the vicarious source of its own excellence, then assumes a solemn and incomprehensible immediacy, as if its decrees were absolute and intrinsically authoritative, not of to-day or yesterday, and no one could tell whence they had arisen. Instinct can all the more easily produce this mystification when it calls forth an imaginative activity full of interest and eager passion. This effect is conspicuous in the absolutist conscience, both devotional and rationalistic, as also in the passion of love. For in all these a certain individuality, definiteness, and exclusiveness is given to the pursued object which is very favourable to zeal, and the heat of passion melts together the various processes of volition into the consciousness of one adorable influence.

However deceptive these complications may prove to men of action and eloquence, they ought not to impose on the critic of human nature. Evidently what value general goods do not derive from the particular satisfactions they stand for, they possess in themselves as ideas pleasing and powerful over the imagination. This intrinsic advantage of certain principles and methods is none the less real for being in a sense æsthetic. Only a sordid utilitarianism that subtracts the imagination from human nature, or at least slurs over its immense contribution to our happiness, could fail to give these principles the preference over others practically as good.

If it could be shown, for instance, that monarchy was as apt, in a given case, to secure the public well-being as some other form of government, monarchy should be preferred, and would undoubtedly be established, on account of its imaginative and dramatic superiority. But if, blinded by this somewhat ethereal advantage, a party sacrificed to it important public interests, the injustice would be manifest. In a doubtful case, a nation decides, not without painful conflicts, how much it will sacrifice to its sentimental needs. The important point is to remember that the representative or practical value of a principle is one thing, and its intrinsic or æsthetic value is another, and that the latter can be justly counted only as an item in its favour to be weighed against possible external disadvantages. Whenever this comparison and balancing of ultimate benefits of every kind is angrily dismissed in favour of some absolute principle, laid down in contempt of human misery and happiness, we have a personal and fantastic system of ethics, without practical sanctions. It is an evidence that the superstitious imagination has invaded the sober and practical domain of morals.

§ 7. ÆSTHETIC AND PHYSICAL PLEASURE. We have now separated with some care intellectual and moral judgments from the sphere of our subject, and found that we are to deal only with perceptions of value, and with these only when they are positive and immediate. But even with these distinctions the most remarkable characteristic of the sense of beauty remains undefined. All pleasures are intrinsic and positive values, but all pleasures are not perceptions of beauty. Pleasure is indeed the essence of that perception, but there is evidently in this particular pleasure a complication which is not present in others and which is the basis of the distinction made by consciousness and language between it and the rest. It will be instructive to notice the degrees of this difference.

The bodily pleasures are those least resembling perceptions of beauty. By bodily pleasures we mean, of course, more than pleasures with a bodily seat; for that class would include them all, as well as all forms and elements of consciousness. Æsthetic pleasures have physical conditions, they depend on the activity of the eye and the ear, of the memory and the other ideational functions of the brain. But we do not connect those pleasures with their seats except in physiological studies; the ideas with which æsthetic pleasures are associated are not the ideas of their bodily causes. The pleasures we call physical, and regard as low, on the contrary, are those which call our attention to some part of our own body, and which make no object so conspicuous to us as the organ in which they arise.

There is here, then, a very marked distinction between physical and æsthetic pleasure; the organs of the latter must be transparent, they must not intercept our attention, but carry it directly to some external object. The greater dignity and range of æsthetic pleasure is thus made very intelligible. The soul is glad, as it were, to forget its connexion with the body and to fancy that it can travel over the world with the liberty with which it changes the objects of its thought. The mind passes from China to Peru without any conscious change in the local tensions of the body. This illusion of disembodiment is very exhilarating, while immersion in the flesh and confinement to some organ gives a tone of grossness and selfishness to our consciousness. The generally meaner associations of physical pleasures also help to explain their comparative crudity.

§ 8. THE DIFFERENTIA OF ÆSTHETIC PLEASURE NOT ITS DISINTERESTEDNESS. The distinction between pleasure and the sense of beauty has sometimes been said to consist in the unselfishness of æsthetic satisfaction. In other pleasures, it is said, we gratify our senses and passions; in the contemplation of beauty we are raised above ourselves, the passions are silenced and we are happy in the recognition of a good that we do not seek to possess. The painter does not look at a spring of water with the eyes of a thirsty man, nor at a beautiful woman with those of a satyr. The difference lies, it is urged, in the impersonality of the enjoyment. But this distinction is one of intensity and delicacy, not of nature, and it seems satisfactory only to the least æsthetic minds.[1]

---

[1] Schopenhauer, indeed, who makes much of it, was a good critic, but his psychology suffered much from the pessimistic generalities of his system. It concerned him to show that the will was bad, and, as he felt beauty to be a good if not a holy thing, he hastened to convince himself that it came from the suppression of the will. But even in his system this suppression is only relative. The desire of individual objects, indeed, is absent in the perception of beauty, but there is still present that initial love of the general type and principles of things which is the first illusion of the absolute,

In the second place, the supposed disinterestedness of æsthetic delights is not very fundamental. Appreciation of a picture is not identical with the desire to buy it, but it is, or ought to be, closely related and preliminary to that desire. The beauties of nature and of the plastic arts are not consumed by being enjoyed; they retain all the efficacy to impress a second beholder. But this circumstance is accidental, and those æsthetic objects which depend upon change and are exhausted in time, as are all performances, are things the enjoyment of which is an object of rivalry and is coveted as much as any other pleasure. And even plastic beauties can often not be enjoyed except by a few, on account of the necessity of travel or other difficulties of access, and then this æsthetic enjoyment is as selfishly pursued as the rest.

The truth which the theory is trying to state seems rather to be that when we seek æsthetic pleasures we have no further pleasure in mind; that we do not mix up the satisfactions of vanity and proprietorship with the delight of contemplation. This is true, but it is true at bottom of all pursuits and enjoyments. Every real pleasure is in one sense disinterested. It is not sought with ulterior motives, and what fills the mind is no calculation, but the image of an object or event, suffused with emotion. A sophisticated consciousness may often take the idea of self as the touchstone of its inclinations; but this self, for the gratification and aggrandizement of which a man may live, is itself only a complex of aims and memories, which once had their direct objects, in which he had taken a spontaneous and unselfish interest. The gratifications which, merged together, make the selfishness are each of them ingenuous, and no more selfish than the most altruistic, impersonal emotion. The content of selfishness is a mass of unselfishness. There is no reference to the nominal essence called oneself either in one's appetites or in one's natural affections; yet a man absorbed in his meat and drink, in his houses and lands, in his children and dogs, is called selfish because these interests, although natural and instinctive in him, are not shared by others. The unselfish man is he whose nature has a more universal direction, whose interests are more widely diffused.

and drives it on to the fatal experiment of creation. So that, apart from Schopenhauer's mythology, we have even in him the recognition that beauty gives satisfaction to some dim and underlying demand of our nature, just as particular objects give more special and momentary pleasures to our individualized wills. His psychology was, however, far too vague and general to undertake an analysis of those mysterious feelings.

But as impersonal thoughts are such only in their object, not in their subject or agent, since all thoughts are the thoughts of somebody: so also unselfish interests have to be somebody's interests. If we were not interested in beauty, if it were of no concern to our happiness whether things were beautiful or ugly, we should manifest not the maximum, but the total absence of æsthetic faculty. The disinterestedness of this pleasure is, therefore, that of all primitive and intuitive satisfactions, which are in no way conditioned by a reference to an artificial general concept, like that of the self, all the potency of which must itself be derived from the independent energy of its component elements. I care about myself because "myself" is a name for the things I have at heart. To set up the verbal figment of personality and make it an object of concern apart from the interests which were its content and substance, turns the moralist into a pedant, and ethics into a superstition. The self which is the object of *amour propre* is an idol of the tribe, and needs to be disintegrated into the primitive objective interests that underlie it before the cultus of it can be justified by reason.

§ 9. THE DIFFERENTIA OF ÆSTHETIC PLEASURE NOT ITS UNIVERSALITY. The supposed disinterestedness of our love of beauty passes into another characteristic of it often regarded as essential, —its universality. The pleasures of the senses have, it is said, no dogmatism in them; that anything gives me pleasure involves no assertion about its capacity to give pleasure to another. But when I judge a thing to be beautiful, my judgment means that the thing is beautiful in itself, or (what is the same thing more critically expressed) that it should seem so to everybody. The claim to universality is, according to this doctrine, the essence of the æsthetic; what makes the perception of beauty a judgment rather than a sensation. All æsthetic precepts would be impossible, and all criticism arbitrary and subjective, unless we admit a paradoxical universality in our judgment, the philosophical implications of which we may then go on to develope. But we are fortunately not required to enter the labyrinth into which this method leads; there is a much simpler and clearer way of studying such questions, which is to challenge and analyze the assertion before us and seek its basis in human nature. Before this is done, we should run the risk of expanding a natural misconception or inaccuracy of thought into an inveterate and pernicious prejudice by making it the centre of an elaborate construction.

That the claim of universality is such a natural inaccuracy will not be hard to show. There is notoriously no great agreement upon æsthetic matters; and such agreement as there is, is based upon similarity of origin, nature, and circumstance among men, a similarity which, where it exists, tends to bring about identity in all judgments and feelings. It is unmeaning to say that what is beautiful to one man *ought* to be beautiful to another. If their senses are the same, their associations and dispositions similar, then the same thing will certainly be beautiful to both. If their natures are different, the form which to one will be entrancing will be to another even invisible, because his classifications and discriminations in perception will be different, and he may see a hideous detached fragment or a shapeless aggregate of things, in what to another is a perfect whole—so entirely are the unities of objects unities of function and use. It is absurd to say that what is invisible to a given being *ought* to seem beautiful to him. Evidently this obligation of recognizing the same qualities is conditioned by the possession of the same faculties. But no two men have exactly the same faculties, nor can things have for any two exactly the same values.

What is loosely expressed by saying that any one ought to see this or that beauty is that he would see it if his disposition, training, or attention were what our ideal demands for him; and our ideal of what any one should be has complex but discoverable sources. We take, for instance, a certain pleasure in having our own judgments supported by those of others; we are intolerant, if not of the existence of a nature different from our own, at least of its expression in words and judgments. We are confirmed or made happy in our doubtful opinions by seeing them accepted universally. We are unable to find the basis of our taste in our own experience and therefore refuse to look for it there. If we were sure of our ground, we should be willing to acquiesce in the naturally different feelings and ways of others, as a man who is conscious of speaking his language with the accent of the capital confesses its arbitrariness with gayety, and is pleased and interested in the variations of it he observes in provincials; but the provincial is always zealous to show that he has reason and ancient authority to justify his oddities. So people who have no sensations, and do not know why they judge, are always trying to show that they judge by universal reason.

Thus the frailty and superficiality of our own judgments cannot brook contradiction. We abhor another man's doubt when

we cannot tell him why we ourselves believe. Our ideal of other
men tends therefore to include the agreement of their judgments with our own; and although we might acknowledge the
fatuity of this demand in regard to natures very different from
the human, we may be unreasonable enough to require that all
races should admire the same style of architecture, and all ages
the same poets.

The great actual unity of human taste within the range of
conventional history helps the pretension. But in principle it is
untenable. Nothing has less to do with the real merit of a work
of imagination than the capacity of all men to appreciate it; the
true test is the degree and kind of satisfaction it can give to him
who appreciates it most. The symphony would lose nothing if
half mankind had always been deaf, as nine-tenths of them
actually are to the intricacies of its harmonies; but it would have
lost much if no Beethoven had existed. And more: incapacity to
appreciate certain types of beauty may be the condition *sine qua
non* for the appreciation of another kind; the greatest capacity
both for enjoyment and creation is highly specialized and
exclusive, and hence the greatest ages of art have often been
strangely intolerant.

The invectives of one school against another, perverse as they
are philosophically, are artistically often signs of health, because
they indicate a vital appreciation of certain kinds of beauty, a
love of them that has grown into a jealous passion. The architects that have pieced out the imperfections of ancient buildings
with their own thoughts, like Charles V. when he raised his
massive palace beside the Alhambra, may be condemned from
a certain point of view. They marred much by their interference;
but they showed a splendid confidence in their own intuitions,
a proud assertion of their own taste, which is the greatest evidence of æsthetic sincerity. On the contrary, our own gropings,
eclecticism, and archæology are the symptoms of impotence. If
we were less learned and less just, we might be more efficient. If
our appreciation were less general, it might be more real, and
if we trained our imagination into exclusiveness, it might attain
to character.

§ 10. THE DIFFERENTIA OF ÆSTHETIC PLEASURE: ITS OBJECTIFICA-
TION. There is, however, something more in the claim to universality in æsthetic judgments than the desire to generalize our
own opinions. There is the expression of a curious but well-
known psychological phenomenon, viz., the transformation of

an element of sensation into the quality of a thing. If we say that other men should see the beauties we see, it is because we think those beauties *are in the object,* like its colour, proportion, or size. Our judgment appears to us merely the perception and discovery of an external existence, of the real excellence that is without. But this notion is radically absurd and contradictory. Beauty, as we have seen, is a value; it cannot be conceived as an independent existence which affects our senses and which we consequently perceive. It exists in perception, and cannot exist otherwise. A beauty not perceived is a pleasure not felt, and a contradiction. But modern philosophy has taught us to say the same thing of every element of the perceived world; all are sensations; and their grouping into objects imagined to be permanent and external is the work of certain habits of our intelligence. We should be incapable of surveying or retaining the diffused experiences of life, unless we organized and classified them, and out of the chaos of impressions framed the world of conventional and recognizable objects.

How this is done is explained by the current theories of perception. External objects usually affect various senses at once, the impressions of which are thereby associated. Repeated experiences of one object are also associated on account of their similarity; hence a double tendency to merge and unify into a single percept, to which a name is attached, the group of those memories and reactions which in fact had one external thing for their cause. But this percept, once formed, is clearly different from those particular experiences out of which it grew. It is permanent, they are variable. They are but partial views and glimpses of it. The constituted notion therefore comes to be the reality, and the materials of it merely the appearance. The distinction between substance and quality, reality and appearance, matter and mind, has no other origin.

The objects thus conceived and distinguished from our ideas of them, are at first compacted of all the impressions, feelings, and memories, which offer themselves for association and fall within the vortex of the amalgamating imagination. Every sensation we get from a thing is originally treated as one of its qualities. Experiment, however, and the practical need of a simpler conception of the structure of objects lead us gradually to reduce the qualities of the object to a minimum, and to regard most perceptions as an effect of those few qualities upon us. These few primary qualities, like extension which we persist in treating as independently real and as the quality of a substance, are those which suffice to explain the order of our experiences. All the rest, like colour, are relegated to the subjective sphere, as merely effects upon our minds, and apparent or secondary qualities of the object.

But this distinction has only a practical justification. Convenience and economy of thought alone determine what combination of our sensations we shall continue to objectify and treat as the cause of the rest. The right and tendency to be objective is equal in all, since they are all prior to the artifice of thought by which we separate the concept from its materials, the thing from our experiences.

The qualities which we now conceive to belong to real objects are for the most part images of sight and touch. One of the first classes of effects to be treated as secondary were naturally pleasures and pains, since it could commonly conduce very little to intelligent and successful action to conceive our pleasures and pains as resident in objects. But emotions are essentially capable of objectification, as well as impressions of sense; and one may well believe that a primitive and inexperienced consciousness would rather people the world with ghosts of its own terrors and passions than with projections of those luminous and mathematical concepts which as yet it could hardly have formed.

This animistic and mythological habit of thought still holds its own at the confines of knowledge, where mechanical explanations are not found. In ourselves, where nearness makes observation difficult, in the intricate chaos of animal and human life, we still appeal to the efficacy of will and ideas, as also in the remote night of cosmic and religious problems. But in all the intermediate realm of vulgar day, where mechanical science has made progress, the inclusion of emotional or passionate elements in the concept of the reality would be now an extravagance. Here our idea of things is composed exclusively of perceptual elements, of the ideas of form and of motion.

The beauty of objects, however, forms an exception to this rule. Beauty is an emotional element, a pleasure of ours, which nevertheless we regard as a quality of things. But we are now prepared to understand the nature of this exception. It is the survival of a tendency originally universal to make every effect of a thing upon us a constituent of its conceived nature. The scientific idea of a thing is a great abstraction from the mass of perceptions and reactions which that thing produces; the æsthetic idea is less abstract, since it retains the emotional reaction, the pleasure of the perception, as an integral part of the conceived thing.

Nor is it hard to find the ground of this survival in the sense of beauty of an objectification of feeling elsewhere extinct. Most of the pleasures which objects cause are easily distinguished and separated from the perception of the object: the object has to be applied to a particular organ, like the palate, or swallowed like wine, or used and operated upon in some way before the pleasure arises. The cohesion is therefore slight between the pleasure and the other associated elements of sense; the pleasure is separated in time from the perception, or it is localized in a different organ, and consequently is at once recognized as an effect and not as a quality of the object. But when the process of perception itself is pleasant, as it may easily be, when the intellectual operation, by which the elements of sense are associated and projected, and the concept of the form and substance of the thing produced, is naturally delightful, then we have a pleasure intimately bound up in the thing, inseparable from its character and constitution, the seat of which in us is the same as the seat of the perception. We naturally fail, under these circumstances, to separate the pleasure from the other objectified feelings. It becomes, like them, a quality of the object, which we distinguish from pleasures not so incorporated in the perception of things, by giving it the name of beauty.

§ 11. THE DEFINITION OF BEAUTY. We have now reached our definition of beauty, which, in the terms of our successive analysis and narrowing of the conception, is value positive, intrinsic, and objectified. Or, in less technical language, Beauty is pleasure regarded as the quality of a thing.

This definition is intended to sum up a variety of distinctions and identifications which should perhaps be here more explicitly set down. Beauty is a value, that is, it is not a perception of a matter of fact or of a relation: it is an emotion, an affection of our volitional and appreciative nature. An object cannot be beautiful if it can give pleasure to nobody: a beauty to which all men were forever indifferent is a contradiction in terms.

In the second place, this value is positive, it is the sense of the presence of something good, or (in the case of ugliness) of its absence. It is never the perception of a positive evil, it is never a negative value. That we are endowed with the sense of beauty is a pure gain which brings no evil with it. When the ugly ceases to be amusing or merely uninteresting and becomes disgusting, it becomes indeed a positive evil: but a moral and practical, not an æsthetic one. In æsthetics that saying is true—often so disingenuous in ethics—that evil is nothing but the absence of good: for even the tedium and vulgarity of an existence without beauty is not itself ugly so much as lamentable and degrading. The absence of æsthetic goods is a moral evil: the æsthetic evil is merely relative, and means less of æsthetic good than was expected at the place and time. No form in itself gives pain, although some forms give pain by causing a shock of surprise even when they are really beautiful: as if a mother found a fine bull pup in her child's cradle, when her pain would not be æsthetic in its nature.

Further, this pleasure must not be in the consequence of the utility of the object or event, but in its immediate perception; in other words, beauty is an ultimate good, something that gives satisfaction to a natural function, to some fundamental need or capacity of our minds. Beauty is therefore a positive value that is intrinsic; it is a pleasure. These two circumstances sufficiently separate the sphere of æsthetics from that of ethics. Moral values are generally negative, and always remote. Morality has to do with the avoidance of evil and the pursuit of good: æsthetics only with enjoyment.

Finally, the pleasures of sense are distinguished from the perception of beauty, as sensation in general is distinguished from perception; by the objectification of the elements and their appearance as qualities rather of things than of consciousness. The passage from sensation to perception is gradual, and the path may be sometimes retraced: so it is with beauty and the pleasures of sensation. There is no sharp line between them, but it depends upon the degree of objectivity my feeling has attained at the moment whether I say "It pleases me," or "It is beautiful." If I am self-conscious and critical, I shall probably use one phrase; if I am impulsive and susceptible, the other. The more remote, interwoven, and inextricable the pleasure is, the more objective it will appear; and the union of two pleasures often makes one beauty. In Shakespeare's LIVth sonnet are these words:

> O how much more doth beauty beauteous seem
> By that sweet ornament which truth doth give!
> The rose looks fair, but fairer we it deem
> For that sweet odour which doth in it live.
> The canker-blooms have full as deep a dye
> As the perfumèd tincture of the roses,
> Hang on such thorns, and play as wantonly

When summer's breath their maskèd buds discloses.
But, for their beauty only is their show,
They live unwooed and unrespected fade;
Die to themselves. Sweet roses do not so:
Of their sweet deaths are sweetest odours made.

One added ornament, we see, turns the deep dye, which was but show and mere sensation before, into an element of beauty and reality; and as truth is here the co-operation of perceptions, so beauty is the co-operation of pleasures. If colour, form, and motion are hardly beautiful without the sweetness of the odour, how much more necessary would they be for the sweetness itself to become a beauty! If we had the perfume in a flask, no one would think of calling it beautiful: it would give us too detached and controllable a sensation. There would be no object in which it could be easily incorporated. But let it float from the garden, and it will add another sensuous charm to objects simultaneously recognized, and help to make them beautiful. Thus beauty is constituted by the objectification of pleasure. It is pleasure objectified.

PART II

THE MATERIALS OF BEAUTY

§ 12. ALL HUMAN FUNCTIONS MAY CONTRIBUTE TO THE SENSE OF BEAUTY. Our task will now be to pass in review the various elements of our consciousness, and see what each contributes to the beauty of the world. We shall find that they do so whenever they are inextricably associated with the objectifying activity of the understanding. Whenever the golden thread of pleasure enters that web of things which our intelligence is always busily spinning, it lends to the visible world that mysterious and subtle charm which we call beauty.

There is no function of our nature which cannot contribute something to this effect, but one function differs very much from another in the amount and directness of its contribution. The pleasures of the eye and ear, of the imagination and memory, are the most easily objectified and merged in ideas; but it would betray inexcusable haste and slight appreciation of the principle involved, if we called them the only materials of beauty. Our effort will rather be to discover its other sources, which have been more generally ignored, and point out their importance. For the five senses and the three powers of the soul, which play so large a part in traditional psychology, are by no means the only sources or factors of consciousness; they are more or less external divisions of its content, and not even exhaustive of that. The nature and changes of our life have deeper roots, and are controlled by less obvious processes.

The human body is a machine that holds together by virtue of certain vital functions, on the cessation of which it is dissolved. Some of these, like the circulation of the blood, the growth and decay of the tissues, are at first sight unconscious. Yet any important disturbance of these fundamental processes at once produces great and painful changes in consciousness. Slight alterations are not without their conscious echo: and the whole temper and tone of our mind, the strength of our passions, the grip and concatenation of our habits, our power of

35

attention, and the liveliness of our fancy and affections are due
to the influence of these vital forces. They do not, perhaps, constitute the whole basis of any one idea or emotion: but they are
the conditions of the existence and character of all.

Particularly important are they for the *value* of our experience. They constitute health, without which no pleasure can
be pure. They determine our impulses in leisure, and furnish
that surplus energy which we spend in play, in art, and in
speculation. The attraction of these pursuits, and the very existence of an æsthetic sphere, is due to the efficiency and perfection of our vital processes. The pleasures which they involve are
not exclusively bound to any particular object, and therefore do
not account for the relative beauty of things. They are loose and
unlocalized, having no special organ, or one which is internal
and hidden within the body. They therefore remain undiscrim-
inated in consciousness, and can serve to add interest to any
object, or to cast a general glamour over the world, very favourable to its interest and beauty.

The æsthetic value of vital functions differs according to their
physiological concomitants: those that are favourable to ideation
are of course more apt to extend something of their intimate
warmth to the pleasures of contemplation, and thus to intensify
the sense of beauty and the interest of thought. Those, on the
other hand, that for physiological reasons tend to inhibit ideation, and to drown the attention in dumb and unrepresentable feelings, are less favourable to æsthetic activity. The
double effect of drowsiness and reverie will illustrate this
difference. The heaviness of sleep seems to fall first on the outer
senses, and of course makes them incapable of acute impressions;
but if it goes no further, it leaves the imagination all the freer,
and by heightening the colours of the fancy, often suggests and
reveals beautiful images. There is a kind of poetry and invention
that comes only in such moments. In them many lovely melodies
must first have been heard, and centaurs and angels originally
imagined.

If, however, the lethargy is more complete, or if the cause of
it is such that the imagination is retarded while the senses remain awake,—as is the case with an over-fed or over-exercised
body,—we have a state of æsthetic insensibility. The exhilaration
which comes with pure and refreshing air has a marked influence
on our appreciations. To it is largely due the beauty of the
morning, and the entirely different charm it has from the
evening. The opposite state of all the functions here adds an

opposite emotion to externally similar scenes, making both infinitely but differently beautiful.

It would be curious and probably surprising to discover how much the pleasure of breathing has to do with our highest and most transcendental ideals. It is not merely a metaphor that makes us couple airiness with exquisiteness and breathlessness with awe; it is the actual recurrence of a sensation in the throat and lungs that gives those impressions an immediate power, prior to all reflection upon their significance. It is, therefore, to this vital sensation of deep or arrested respiration that the impressiveness of those objects is immediately due.

§ 13. THE INFLUENCE OF THE PASSION OF LOVE. Half-way between vital and social functions, lies the sexual instinct. If nature had solved the problem of reproduction without the differentiation of sex, our emotional life would have been radically different. So profound and, especially in woman, so pervasive an influence does this function exert, that we should betray an entirely unreal view of human nature if we did not inquire into the relations of sex with our æsthetic susceptibility. We must not expect, however, any great difference between man and woman in the scope or objects of æsthetic interest: what is important in emotional life is not which sex an animal has, but that it has sex at all. For if we consider the difficult problem which nature had to solve in sexual reproduction, and the nice adjustment of instinct which it demands, we shall see that the reactions and susceptibilities which must be implanted in the individual are for the most part identical in both sexes, as the sexual organization is itself fundamentally similar in both. Indeed, individuals of various species and the whole animal kingdom have the same sexual disposition, although, of course, the particular object destined to call forth the complete sexual reaction, differs with every species, and with each sex.

If we were dealing with the philosophy of love, and not with that of beauty, our problem would be to find out by what machinery this fundamental susceptibility, common to all animals of both sexes, is gradually directed to more and more definite objects: first, to one species and one sex, and ultimately to one individual. It is not enough that sexual organs should be differentiated: the connexion must be established between them and the outer senses, so that the animal may recognize and pursue the proper object.

The case of lifelong fidelity to one mate—perhaps even to an unsatisfied and hopeless love—is the maximum of differentiation, which even overleaps the utility which gave it a foothold in nature, and defeats its own object. For the differentiation of the instinct in respect to sex, age, and species is obviously necessary to its success as a device for reproduction. While this differentiation is not complete,—and it often is not,—there is a great deal of groping and waste; and the force and constancy of the instinct must make up for its lack of precision. A great deal of vital energy is thus absorbed by this ill-adjusted function. The most economical arrangement which can be conceived, would be one by which only the one female best fitted to bear offspring to a male should arouse his desire, and only so many times as it was well she should grow pregnant, thus leaving his energy and attention free at all other times to exercise the other faculties of his nature.

If this ideal had been reached, the instinct, like all those perfectly adjusted, would tend to become unconscious; and we should miss those secondary effects with which we are exclusively concerned in æsthetics. For it is precisely from the waste, from the radiation of the sexual passion, that beauty borrows warmth. As a harp, made to vibrate to the fingers, gives some music to every wind, so the nature of man, necessarily susceptible to woman, becomes simultaneously sensitive to other influences, and capable of tenderness toward every object. The capacity to love gives our contemplation that glow without which it might often fail to manifest beauty; and the whole sentimental side of our æsthetic sensibility—without which it would be perceptive and mathematical rather than æsthetic—is due to our sexual organization remotely stirred.

The attraction of sex could not become efficient unless the senses were first attracted. The eye must be fascinated and the ear charmed by the object which nature intends should be pursued. Both sexes for this reason develope secondary sexual characteristics; and the sexual emotions are simultaneously extended to various secondary objects. The colour, the grace, the form, which become the stimuli of sexual passion, and the guides of sexual selection, acquire, before they can fulfil that office, a certain intrinsic charm. This charm is not only present for reasons which, in an admissible sense, we may call teleological, on account, that is, of its past utility in reproduction, but its intensity and power are due to the simultaneous stirring of profound sexual impulses. Not, of course, that any specifically sexual ideas are connected with these feelings: such ideas are absent in a modest and inexperienced mind even in the obviously sexual passions of love and jealousy.

These secondary objects of interest, which are some of the most conspicuous elements of beauty, are to be called sexual for these two reasons: because the contingencies of the sexual function have helped to establish them in our race, and because they owe their fascination in a great measure to the participation of our sexual life in the reaction which they cause.

If any one were desirous to produce a being with a great susceptibility to beauty, he could not invent an instrument better designed for that object than sex. Individuals that need not unite for the birth and rearing of each generation, might retain a savage independence. For them it would not be necessary that any vision should fascinate, or that any languor should soften, the prying cruelty of the eye. But sex endows the individual with a dumb and powerful instinct, which carries his body and soul continually towards another; makes it one of the dearest employments of his life to select and pursue a companion, and joins to possession the keenest pleasure, to rivalry the fiercest rage, and to solitude an eternal melancholy.

What more could be needed to suffuse the world with the deepest meaning and beauty? The attention is fixed upon a well-defined object, and all the effects it produces in the mind are easily regarded as powers or qualities of that object. But these effects are here powerful and profound. The soul is stirred to its depths. Its hidden treasures are brought to the surface of consciousness. The imagination and the heart awake for the first time. All these new values crystallize about the objects then offered to the mind. If the fancy is occupied by the image of a single person, whose qualities have had the power of precipitating this revolution, all the values gather about that one image. The object becomes perfect, and we are said to be in love.[1] If the stimulus does not appear as a definite image, the values evoked are dispersed over the world, and we are said to have become lovers of nature, and to have discovered the beauty and meaning of things.

To a certain extent this kind of interest will centre in the proper object of sexual passion, and in the special characteristics of the opposite sex; and we find accordingly that woman is the most lovely object to man, and man, if female modesty would confess it, the most interesting to woman. But the effects

[1] Cf. Stendhal, *De l'Amour, passim.*

of so fundamental and primitive a reaction are much more general. Sex is not the only object of sexual passion. When love lacks its specific object, when it does not yet understand itself, or has been sacrificed to some other interest, we see the stifled fire bursting out in various directions. One is religious devotion, another is zealous philanthropy, a third is the fondling of pet animals, but not the least fortunate is the love of nature, and of art; for nature also is often a second mistress that consoles us for the loss of a first. Passion then overflows and visibly floods those neighbouring regions which it had always secretly watered. For the same nervous organization which sex involves, with its necessarily wide branchings and associations in the brain, must be partially stimulated by other objects than its specific or ultimate one; especially in man, who, unlike some of the lower animals, has not his instincts clearly distinct and intermittent, but always partially active, and never active in isolation. We may say, then, that for man all nature is a secondary object of sexual passion, and that to this fact the beauty of nature is largely due.

§ 14. SOCIAL INSTINCTS AND THEIR ÆSTHETIC INFLUENCE. The function of reproduction carries with it not only direct modifications of the body and mind, but a whole set of social institutions, for the existence of which social instincts and habits are necessary in man. These social feelings, the parental, the patriotic, or the merely gregarious, are not of much direct value for æsthetics, although, as is seen in the case of fashions, they are important in determining the duration and prevalence of a taste once formed. Indirectly they are of vast importance and play a great rôle in arts like poetry, where the effect depends on what is signified more than on what is offered to sense. Any appeal to a human interest rebounds in favour of a work of art in which it is successfully made. That interest, unæsthetic in itself, helps to fix the attention and to furnish subject-matter and momentum to arts and modes of appreciation which are æsthetic. Thus comprehension of the passion of love is necessary to the appreciation of numberless songs, plays, and novels, and not a few works of musical and plastic art.

The treatment of these matters must be postponed until we are prepared to deal with expression—the most complex element of effect. It will suffice here to point out why social and gregarious impulses, in the satisfaction of which happiness mainly resides, are those in which beauty finds least support. This may help us to understand better the relations between æsthetics and *hedonics,* and the nature of that objectification in which we have placed the difference between beauty and pleasure.

So long as happiness is conceived as a poet might conceive it, namely, in its immediately sensuous and emotional factors, so long as we live in the moment and make our happiness consist in the simplest things,—in breathing, seeing, hearing, loving, and sleeping,—our happiness has the same substance, the same elements, as our æsthetic delight, for it is æsthetic delight that makes our happiness. Yet poets and artists, with their immediate and æsthetic joys, are not thought to be happy men; they themselves are apt to be loud in their lamentations, and to regard themselves as eminently and tragically unhappy. This arises from the intensity and inconstancy of their emotions, from their improvidence, and from the eccentricity of their social habits. While among them the sensuous and vital functions have the upper hand, the gregarious and social instincts are subordinated and often deranged; and their unhappiness consists in the sense of their unfitness to live in the world into which they are born.

But man is pre-eminently a political animal, and social needs are almost as fundamental in him as vital functions, and often more conscious. Friendship, wealth, reputation, power, and influence, when added to family life, constitute surely the main elements of happiness. Now these are only very partially composed of definite images of objects. The desire for them, the consciousness of their absence or possession, comes upon us only when we reflect, when we are planning, considering the future, gathering the words of others, rehearsing their scorn or admiration for ourselves, conceiving possible situations in which our virtue, our fame or power would become conspicuous, comparing our lot with that of others, and going through other discursive processes of thought. Apprehension, doubt, isolation, are things which come upon us keenly when we reflect upon our lives; they cannot easily become qualities of any object. If by chance they can, they acquire a great æsthetic value. For instance, "home," which in its social sense is a concept of happiness, when it becomes materialized in a cottage and a garden becomes an æsthetic concept, becomes a beautiful thing. The happiness is objectified, and the object beautified.

Social objects, however, are seldom thus æsthetic, because they are not thus definitely imaginable. They are diffuse and abstract, and verbal rather than sensuous in their materials. Therefore the great emotions that go with them are not immediately transmutable into beauty. If artists and poets are unhappy, it is after all because happiness does not interest them. They cannot seriously pursue it, because its components are not components of beauty, and being in love with beauty, they neglect and despise those unæsthetic social virtues in the operation of which happiness is found. On the other hand those who pursue happiness conceived merely in the abstract and conventional terms, as money, success, or respectability, often miss that real and fundamental part of happiness which flows from the senses and imagination. This element is what æsthetics supplies to life; for beauty also can be a cause and a factor of happiness. Yet the happiness of loving beauty is either too sensuous to be stable, or else too ultimate, too sacramental, to be accounted happiness by the worldly mind.

§ 15. THE LOWER SENSES. The senses of touch, taste, and smell, although capable no doubt of a great development, have not served in man for the purposes of intelligence so much as those of sight and hearing. It is natural that as they remain normally in the background of consciousness, and furnish the least part of our objectified ideas, the pleasures connected with them should remain also detached, and unused for the purpose of appreciation of nature. They have been called the unæsthetic, as well as the lower, senses; but the propriety of these epithets, which is undeniable, is due not to any intrinsic sensuality or baseness of these senses, but to the function which they happen to have in our experience. Smell and taste, like hearing, have the great disadvantage of not being intrinsically spatial: they are therefore not fitted to serve for the representation of nature, which allows herself to be accurately conceived only in spatial terms.[1] They have not reached, moreover, the same organization as sounds, and therefore cannot furnish any play of subjective sensation comparable to music in interest.

The objectification of musical forms is due to their fixity and complexity: like words, they are thought of as existing in a social medium, and can be beautiful without being spatial. But tastes have never been so accurately or universally classified and distinguished; the instrument of sensation does not allow such

[1] This is not the place to enter into a discussion of the metaphysical value of the idea of space. Suffice it to point out that in human experience serviceable knowledge of our environment is to be had only in spatial symbols, and, for whatever reason or accident, this is the language which the mind must speak if it is to advance in clearness and efficiency.

nice and stable discriminations as does the ear. The art of com-
bining dishes and wines, although one which everybody practises
with more or less skill and attention, deals with a material far
too unrepresentable to be called beautiful. The art remains in
the sphere of the pleasant, and is consequently regarded as
servile, rather than fine.

Artists in life, if that expression may be used for those who
have beautified social and domestic existence, have appealed
continually to these lower senses. A fragrant garden, and savoury
meats, incense, and perfumes, soft stuffs, and delicious colours,
form our ideal of oriental luxuries, an ideal which appeals too
much to human nature ever to lose its charm. Yet our northern
poets have seldom attempted to arouse these images in their
sensuous intensity, without relieving them by some imaginative
touch. In Keats, for example, we find the following lines:—

> And still she slept in azure-lidded sleep,
> In blanched linen, smooth and lavendered,
> While he from forth the closet brought a heap
> Of candied apple, quince, and plum, and gourd,
> With jellies soother than the creamy curd,
> And lucent syrops tinct with cinnamon;
> Manna and dates in argosy transferred
> From Fez; and spiced dainties, every one
> From silken Samarcand to cedared Lebanon.

Even the most sensuous of English poets, in whom the love of
beauty is supreme, cannot keep long to the primal elements of
beauty; the higher flight is inevitable for him. And how much
does not the appeal to things in argosy transferred from Fez,
reinforced with the reference to Samarcand and especially to
the authorized beauties of the cedars of Lebanon, which even
the Puritan may sing without a blush, add to our wavering satisfaction and reconcile our conscience to this unchristian indulgence of sense!

But the time may be near when such scruples will be less
common, and our poetry, with our other arts, will dwell nearer
to the fountain-head of all inspiration. For if nothing not once
in sense is to be found in the intellect, much less is such a thing
to be found in the imagination. If the cedars of Lebanon did
not spread a grateful shade, or the winds rustle through the
maze of their branches, if Lebanon had never been beautiful to
sense, it would not now be a fit or poetic subject of allusion.
And the word "Fez" would be without imaginative value if no
traveller had ever felt the intoxication of the torrid sun, the

languors of oriental luxury, or, like the British soldier, cried amid the dreary moralities of his native land:—

> Take me somewhere east of Suez
>   Where the best is like the worst,
> Where there ain't no ten commandments
>   And a man may raise a thirst.

Nor would Samarcand be anything but for the mystery of the desert and the picturesqueness of caravans, nor would an argosy be poetic if the sea had no voices and no foam, the winds and oars no resistance, and the rudder and taut sheets no pull. From these real sensations imagination draws its life, and suggestion its power. The sweep of the fancy is itself also agreeable; but the superiority of the distant over the present is only due to the mass and variety of the pleasures that can be suggested, compared with the poverty of those that can at any time be felt.

§ 16. SOUND. Sound shares with the lower senses the disadvantage of having no intrinsic spatial character; it, therefore, forms no part of the properly abstracted external world, and the pleasures of the ear cannot become, in the literal sense, qualities of *things*. But there is in sounds such an exquisite and continuous gradation in pitch, and such a measurable relation in length, that an object almost as complex and describable as the visible one can be built out of them. What gives spatial forms their value in description of the environment is the ease with which discriminations and comparisons can be made in spatial objects: they are measurable, while unspatial sensations commonly are not. But sounds are also measurable in their own category: they have comparable pitches and durations, and definite and recognizable combinations of those sensuous elements are as truly *objects* as chairs and tables. Not that a musical composition exists in any mystical way, as a portion of the music of the spheres, which no one is hearing; but that, for a critical philosophy, visible objects are also nothing but possibilities of sensation. The real world is merely the shadow of that assurance of eventual experience which accompanies sanity. This objectivity can accrue to any mental figment that has enough cohesion, content, and individuality to be describable and recognizable, and these qualities belong no less to audible than to spatial ideas.

There is, accordingly, some justification in Schopenhauer's speculative assertion that music repeats the entire world of sense, and is a parallel method of expression of the underlying substance, or will. The world of sound is certainly capable of in-

finite variety and, were our sense developed, of infinite extensions; and it has as much as the world of matter the power to
interest us and to stir our emotions. It was therefore potentially
as full of meaning. But it has proved the less serviceable and
constant apparition; and, therefore, music, which builds with its
materials, while the purest and most impressive of the arts, is
the least human and instructive of them.

The pleasantness of sounds has a simple physical basis. All
sensations are pleasant only between certain limits of intensity;
but the ear can discriminate easily between noises, that in themselves are uninteresting, if not annoying, and notes, which have
an unmistakable charm. A sound is a note if the pulsations of the
air by which it is produced recur at regular intervals. If there
is no regular recurrence of waves, it is a noise. The rapidity of
these regular beats determines the pitch of tones. That quality
or *timbre* by which one sound is distinguished from another
of the same pitch and intensity is due to the different complications of waves in the air; the ability to discriminate the various
waves in the vibrating air is, therefore, the condition of our
finding music in it; for every wave has its period, and what we
call a noise is a complication of notes too complex for our organs
or our attention to decipher.

We find here, at the very threshold of our subject, a clear instance of a conflict of principles which appears everywhere in
æsthetics, and is the source and explanation of many conflicts of
taste. Since a note is heard when a set of regular vibrations can
be discriminated in the chaos of sound, it appears that the perception and value of this artistic element depends on abstraction,
on the omission from the field of attention, of all the elements
which do not conform to a simple law. This may be called the
principle of purity. But if it were the only principle at work,
there would be no music more beautiful than the tone of a
tuning-fork. Such sounds, although delightful perhaps to a child,
are soon tedious. The principle of purity must make some compromise with another principle, which we may call that of interest. The object must have enough variety and expression to
hold our attention for a while, and to stir our nature widely.

As we are more acutely sensitive to results or to processes, we
find the most agreeable effect nearer to one or to the other of
these extremes of a tedious beauty or of an unbeautiful expressiveness. But these principles, as is clear, are not co-ordinate. The
child who enjoys his rattle or his trumpet has æsthetic enjoyment, of however rude a kind; but the master of technique who

should give a performance wholly without sensuous charm would be a gymnast and not a musician, and the author whose novels and poems should be merely expressive, and interesting only by their meaning and moral, would be a writer of history or philosophy, but not an artist. The principle of purity is therefore essential to æsthetic effect, but the principle of interest is subsidiary, and if appealed to alone would fail to produce beauty.

The distinction, however, is not absolute: for the simple sensation is itself interesting, and the complication, if it is appreciable by sense and does not require discursive thought to grasp it, is itself beautiful. There may be a work of art in which the sensuous materials are not pleasing, as a discourse without euphony, if the structure and expression give delight; and there may be an interesting object without perceived structure, like musical notes, or the blue sky. Perfection would, of course, lie in the union of elements all intrinsically beautiful, in forms also intrinsically so; but where this is impossible, different natures prefer to sacrifice one or the other advantage.

§ 17. COLOUR. In the eye we have an organ so differentiated that it is sensitive to a much more subtle influence than even that of air waves. There seems to be, in the interstellar spaces, some pervasive fluid, for the light of the remotest star is rapidly conveyed to us, and we can hardly understand how this radiation of light, which takes place beyond our atmosphere, could be realized without some medium. This hypothetical medium we call the ether. It is capable of very rapid vibrations, which are propagated in all directions, like the waves of sound, only much more quickly. Many common observations, such as the apparent interval between lightning and thunder, make us aware of the quicker motion of light. Now, since nature was filled with this responsive fluid, which propagated to all distances vibrations originating at any point, and moreover as these vibrations, when intercepted by a solid body, were reflected wholly or in part, it obviously became very advantageous to every animal to develope an organ sensitive to these vibrations—sensitive, that is, to light. For this would give the mind instantaneous impressions dependent upon the presence and nature of distant objects.

To this circumstance we must attribute the primacy of sight in our perception, a primacy that makes light the natural symbol of knowledge. When the time came for our intelligence to take the great metaphysical leap, and conceive its content as permanent and independent, or, in other words, to imagine *things,* the idea of these *things* had to be constructed out of the materials already present to the mind. But the fittest material for such construction was that furnished by the eye, since it is the eye that brings us into widest relations with our actual environment, and gives us the quickest warning of approaching impressions. Sight has a prophetic function. We are less interested in it for itself than for the suggestion it brings of what may follow after. Sight is a method of presenting psychically what is practically absent; and as the essence of the *thing* is its existence in our absence, the *thing* is spontaneously conceived in terms of sight.

Sight is, therefore, perception *par excellence,* since we become most easily aware of objects through visual agency and in visual terms. Now, as the values of perception are those we call æsthetic, and there could be no beauty if there was no conception of independent objects, we may expect to find beauty derived mainly from the pleasures of sight. And, in fact, form, which is almost a synonym of beauty, is for us usually something visible: it is a synthesis of the seen. But prior to the effect of form, which arises in the constructive imagination, comes the effect of colour; this is purely sensuous, and no better intrinsically than the effects of any other sense: but being more involved in the perception of objects than are the rest, it becomes more readily an element of beauty.

The values of colours differ appreciably and have analogy to the differing values of other sensations. As sweet or pungent smells, as high and low notes, or major and minor chords, differ from each other by virtue of their different stimulation of the senses, so also red differs from green, and green from violet. There is a nervous process for each, and consequently a specific value. This emotional quality has affinity to the emotional quality of other sensations; we need not be surprised that the high rate of vibration which yields a sharp note to the ear should involve somewhat the same feeling that is produced by the high rate of vibration which, to the eye, yields a violet colour. These affinities escape many minds; but it is conceivable that the sense of them should be improved by accident or training. There are certain effects of colour which give all men pleasure, and others which jar, almost like a musical discord. A more general development of this sensibility would make possible a new abstract art, an art that should deal with colours as music does with sound.

We have not studied these effects, however, with enough attention, we have not allowed them to penetrate enough into the soul, to think them very significant. The stimulation of fire-works, or of kaleidoscopic effects, seems to us trivial. But every-thing which has a varied content has a potentiality of form and also of meaning. The form will be enjoyed as soon as attention accustoms us to discriminate and recognize its variations; and meaning will accrue to it, when the various emotional values of these forms ally the new object to all other experiences which involve similar emotions, and thus give it a sympathetic environ-ment in the mind. The colours of the sunset have a brilliancy that attracts attention, and a softness and illusiveness that en-chant the eye; while the many associations of the evening and of heaven gather about this kindred charm and deepen it. Thus the most sensuous of beauties can be full of sentimental suggestion. In stained glass, also, we have an example of masses of colour made to exert their powerful direct influence, to intensify an emotion eventually to be attached to very ideal objects; what is in itself a gorgeous and unmeaning ornament, by its absolute impressiveness becomes a vivid symbol of those other ultimates which have a similar power over the soul.

§ 18. MATERIALS SURVEYED. We have now gone over those organs of perception that give us the materials out of which we construct objects, and mentioned the most conspicuous pleasures which, as they arise from those organs, are easily merged in the ideas furnished by the same. We have also noticed that these ideas, conspicuous as they are in our developed and operating consciousness, are not so much factors in our thought, independ-ent contributors to it, as they are discriminations and excisions in its content, which, after they are all made, leave still a back-ground of vital feeling. For the outer senses are but a portion of our sensorium, and the ideas of each, or of all together, but a portion of our consciousness.

The pleasures which accompany ideation we have also found to be unitary and vital; only just as for practical purposes it is necessary to abstract and discriminate the contribution of one sense from that of another, and thus to become aware of par-ticular and definable impressions, so it is natural that the dif-fused emotional tone of the body should also be divided, and a certain modicum of pleasure or pain should be attributed to each idea. Our pleasures are thus described as the pleasures of touch, taste, smell, hearing, and sight, and may become elements of beauty at the same time as the ideas to which they are at-tached become elements of objects. There is, however, a remainder of emotion as there is a remainder of sensation; and the importance of this remainder—of the continuum in which lie all particular pleasures and pains—was insisted upon in the beginning.

The beauty of the world, indeed, cannot be attributed wholly or mainly to pleasures thus attached to abstracted sensations. It is only the beauty of the materials of things which is drawn from the pleasures of sensation. By far the most important effects are not attributable to these materials, but to their arrangement and their ideal relations. We have yet to study those processes of our mind by which this arrangement and these relations are conceived; and the pleasures which we can attach to these processes may then be added to the pleasures attached to sense as further and more subtle elements of beauty.

But before passing to the consideration of this more intricate subject, we may note that however subordinate the beauty may be which a garment, a building, or a poem derives from its sensuous material, yet the presence of this sensuous material is indispensable. Form cannot be the form of nothing. If, then, in finding or creating beauty, we ignore the materials of things, and attend only to their form, we miss an ever-present opportunity to heighten our effects. For whatever delight the form may bring, the material might have given delight already, and so much would have been gained towards the value of the total result.

Sensuous beauty is not the greatest or most important element of effect, but it is the most primitive and fundamental, and the most universal. There is no effect of form which an effect of material could not enhance, and this effect of material, underlying that of form, raises the latter to a higher power and gives the beauty of the object a certain poignancy, thoroughness, and infinity which it otherwise would have lacked. The Parthenon not in marble, the king's crown not of gold, and the stars not of fire, would be feeble and prosaic things. The greater hold which material beauty has upon the senses, stimulates us here, where the form is also sublime, and lifts and intensifies our emotions. We need this stimulus if our perceptions are to reach the highest pitch of strength and acuteness. Nothing can be ravishing that is not beautiful pervasively.

And another point. The wider diffusion of sensuous beauty makes it as it were the poor man's good. Fewer factors are needed to produce it and less training to appreciate it. The senses are indispensable instruments of labour, developed by the necessities of life; but their perfect development produces a harmony between the inward structure and instinct of the organ and the outward opportunities for its use; and this harmony is the source of continual pleasures. In the sphere of sense, therefore, a certain cultivation is inevitable in man; often greater, indeed, among rude peoples, perhaps among animals, than among those whose attention takes a wider sweep and whose ideas are more abstract. Without requiring, therefore, that a man should rise above his station, or develope capacities which his opportunities will seldom employ, we may yet endow his life with æsthetic interest, if we allow him the enjoyment of sensuous beauty. This enriches him without adding to his labour, and flatters him without alienating him from his world.

Taste, when it is spontaneous, always begins with the senses. Children and savages, as we are so often told, delight in bright and variegated colours; the simplest people appreciate the neatness of muslin curtains, shining varnish, and burnished pots. A rustic garden is a shallow patchwork of the liveliest flowers, without that reserve and repose which is given by spaces and masses. Noise and vivacity is all that childish music contains, and primitive songs add little more of form than what is required to compose a few monotonous cadences. These limitations are not to be regretted; they are a proof of sincerity. Such simplicity is not the absence of taste, but the beginning of it.

A people with genuine æsthetic perceptions creates traditional forms and expresses the simple pathos of its life, in unchanging but significant themes, repeated by generation after generation. When sincerity is lost, and a snobbish ambition is substituted, bad taste comes in. The essence of it is a substitution of nonæsthetic for æsthetic values. To love glass beads because they are beautiful is barbarous, perhaps, but not vulgar; to love jewels only because they are dear is vulgar, and to betray the motive by placing them ineffectively is an offence against taste. The test is always the same: Does the thing itself actually please? If it does, your taste is real; it may be different from that of others, but is equally justified and grounded in human nature. If it does not, your whole judgment is spurious, and you are guilty, not of heresy, which in æsthetics is orthodoxy itself, but of hypocrisy, which is a self-excommunication from its sphere.

Now, a great sign of this hypocrisy is insensibility to sensuous beauty. When people show themselves indifferent to primary and fundamental effects, when they are incapable of finding pictures except in frames or beauties except in the great masters, we may justly suspect that they are parrots, and that their verbal and historical knowledge covers a natural lack of æsthetic sense. Where, on the contrary, insensibility to higher forms of beauty does not exclude a natural love of the lower, we have every reason to be encouraged; there is a true and healthy taste, which only needs experience to refine it. If a man demands light, sound, and splendour, he proves that he has the æsthetic equilibrium; that appearances as such interest him, and that he can pause in perception to enjoy. We have but to vary his observation, to enlarge his thought, to multiply his discriminations—all of which education can do—and the same æsthetic habit will reveal to him every shade of the fit and fair. Or if it should not, and the man, although sensuously gifted, proved to be imaginatively dull, at least he would not have failed to catch an intimate and widespread element of effect. The beauty of material is thus the groundwork of all higher beauty, both in the object, whose form and meaning have to be lodged in something sensible, and in the mind, where sensuous ideas, being the first to emerge, are the first that can arouse delight.

PART III

FORM

§ 19. THERE IS A BEAUTY OF FORM. The most remarkable and characteristic problem of æsthetics is that of beauty of form. Where there is a sensuous delight, like that of colour, and the impression of the object is in its elements agreeable, we have to look no farther for an explanation of the charm we feel. Where there is expression, and an object indifferent to the senses is associated with other ideas which are interesting, the problem, although complex and varied, is in principle comparatively plain. But there is an intermediate effect which is more mysterious, and more specifically an effect of beauty. It is found where sensible elements, by themselves indifferent, are so united as to please in combination. There is something unexpected in this phenomenon, so much so that those who cannot conceive its explanation often reassure themselves by denying its existence. To reduce beauty of form, however, to beauty of elements would not be easy, because the creation and variation of effect, by changing the relation of the simplest lines, offers too easy an experiment in reputation. And it would, moreover, follow to the comfort of the vulgar that all marble houses are equally beautiful.

To attribute beauty of form to expression is more plausible. If I take the meaningless short lines in the figure and arrange

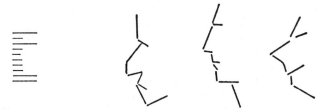

them in the given ways, intended to represent the human face, there appear at once notably different æsthetic values. Two of the forms are differently grotesque and one approximately beautiful. Now these effects are due to the expression of the lines; not only because they make one think of fair or ugly faces, but because, it may be said, these faces would in reality be fair or ugly, according to their expression, according to the vital and moral associations of the different types.

Nevertheless, beauty of form cannot be reduced to expression without denying the existence of immediate æsthetic values altogether, and reducing them all to suggestions of moral good. For if the object expressed by the form, and from which the form derives its value, had itself beauty of form, we should not advance; we must come somewhere to the point where the expression is of something else than beauty; and this something else would of course be some practical or moral good. Moralists are fond of such an interpretation, and it is a very interesting one. It puts beauty in the same relation to morals in which morals stand to pleasure and pain; both would be intuitions, qualitatively new, but with the same materials; they would be new perspectives of the same object.

But this theory is actually inadmissible. Innumerable æsthetic effects, indeed all specific and unmixed ones, are direct transmutations of pleasures and pains; they express nothing extrinsic to themselves, much less moral excellences. The detached lines of our figure signify nothing, but they are not absolutely uninteresting; the straight line is the simplest and not the least beautiful of forms. To say that it owes its interest to the thought of the economy of travelling over the shortest road, or of other practical advantages, would betray a feeble hold on psychological reality. The impression of a straight line differs in a certain almost emotional way from that of a curve, as those of various curves do from one another. The quality of the sensation is different, like that of various colours or sounds. To attribute the character of these forms to association would be like explaining sea-sickness as the fear of shipwreck. There is a distinct quality and value, often a singular beauty, in these simple lines that is intrinsic in the perception of their form.

It would be pedantic, perhaps, anywhere but in a treatise on æsthetics, to deny to this quality the name of expression; we might commonly say that the circle has one expression and the oval another. But what does the circle express except circularity, or the oval except the nature of the ellipse? Such expression *expresses* nothing; it is really *im*pression. There may be analogy between it and other impressions; we may admit that odours, colours, and sounds correspond, and may mutually suggest one another; but this analogy is a superadded charm felt by very sensitive natures, and does not constitute the original value of the sensations. The common emotional tinge is rather what enables them to suggest one another, and what makes them comparable. Their expression, such as it is, is therefore due to the accident that both feelings have a kindred quality; and this quality has its effectiveness for sense independently of the perception of its recurrence in a different sphere. We shall accordingly take care to reserve the term "expression" for the suggestion of some other and assignable object, from which the expressive thing borrows an interest; and we shall speak of the intrinsic quality of forms as their emotional tinge or specific value.

§ 20. PHYSIOLOGY OF THE PERCEPTION OF FORM. The charm of a line evidently consists in the relation of its parts; in order to understand this interest in spatial relations, we must inquire how they are perceived.[1] If the eye had its sensitive surface, the retina, exposed directly to the light, we could never have a perception of form any more than in the nose or ear, which also perceive the object through media. When the perception is not through a medium, but direct, as in the case of the skin, we might get a notion of form, because each point of the object would excite a single point in the skin, and as the sensations in different parts of the skin differ in quality, a manifold of sense, in which discrimination of parts would be involved, could be presented to the mind. But when the perception is through a medium, a difficulty arises.

Any point, *a*, in the object will send a ray to every point, *a'*, *b'*, *c'*, of the sensitive surface; every point of the retina will therefore be similarly affected, since each will receive rays from every

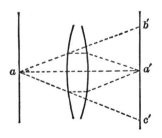

---

[1] The discussion is limited in this chapter to visible form; audible form is probably capable of a parallel treatment, but requires studies too technical for this place.

part of the object. If all the rays from one point of the object, *a*, are to be concentrated on a corresponding point of the retina, *a'*, which would then become the exclusive representative of *a*, we must have one or more refracting surfaces interposed, to gather the rays together. The presence of the lens, with its various coatings, has made representation of point by point possible for the eye. The absence of such an instrument makes the same sort of representation impossible to other senses, such as the nose, which does not smell in one place the effluvia of one part of the environment and in another place the effluvia of another, but smells indiscriminately the combination of all. Eyes without lenses like those possessed by some animals, undoubtedly give only a consciousness of diffused light, without the possibility of boundaries or divisions in the field of view. The abstraction of colour from form is therefore by no means an artificial one, since, by a simplification of the organ of sense, one may be perceived without the other.

But even if the lens enables the eye to receive a distributed image of the object, the manifold which consciousness would perceive would not be necessarily a manifold of parts juxtaposed in space. Each point of the retina might send to the brain a detached impression; these might be comparable, but not necessarily in their spatial position. The ear sends to the brain such a manifold of impressions (since the ear also has an apparatus by which various external differences in rapidity of vibrations are distributed into different parts of the organ). But this discriminated manifold is a manifold of pitches, not of positions. How does it happen that the manifold conveyed by the optic nerve appears in consciousness as spatial, and that the relation between its elements is seen as a relation of position?

An answer to this question has been suggested by various psychologists. The eye, by an instinctive movement, turns so as to bring every impression upon that point of the retina, near its centre, which has the acutest sensibility. A series of muscular sensations therefore always follows upon the conspicuous excitement of any outlying point. The object, as the eye brings it to the centre of vision, excites a series of points upon the retina; and the local sign, or peculiar quality of sensation, proper to each of these spots, is associated with that series of muscular feelings involved in turning the eyes. These feelings henceforth revive together; it is enough that a point in the periphery of the retina should receive a ray, for the mind to feel, together with that impression, the suggestion of a motion, and of the line of points that lies between the excited point and the centre of vision. A network of associations is thus formed, whereby the sensation of each retinal point is connected with all the others in a manner which is that of points in a plane. Every visible point becomes thus a point in a field, and has a felt radiation of lines of possible motion about it. Our notion of visual space has this origin, since the manifold of retinal impressions is distributed in a manner which serves as the type and exemplar of what we mean by a surface.

§ 21. VALUES OF GEOMETRICAL FIGURES. The reader will perhaps pardon these details and the strain they put on his attention, when he perceives how much they help us to understand the value of forms. The sense, then, of the position of any point consists in the tensions in the eye, that not only tends to bring that point to the centre of vision, but feels the suggestion of all the other points which are related to the given one in the web of visual experience. The definition of space as the possibility of motion is therefore an accurate and significant one, since the most direct and native perception of space we can have is the awakening of many tendencies to move our organs.

For example, if a circle is presented, the eye will fall upon its centre, as to the centre of gravity, as it were, of the balanced attractions of all the points; and there will be, in that position, an indifference and sameness of sensation, in whatever direction some accident moves the eye, that accounts very well for the emotional quality of the circle. It is a form which, although beautiful in its purity and simplicity, and wonderful in its continuity, lacks any stimulating quality, and is often ugly in the arts, especially when found in vertical surfaces where it is not always seen in perspective. For horizontal surfaces it is better because it is there always an ellipse to vision, and the ellipse has a less dull and stupefying effect. The eye can move easily, organize and subordinate its parts, and its relations to the environment are not similar in all directions. Small circles, like buttons, are not in the same danger of becoming ugly, because the eye considers them as points, and they diversify and help to divide surfaces, without appearing as surfaces themselves.

The straight line offers a curious object for analysis. It is not for the eye a very easy form to grasp. We bend it or we leave it. Unless it passes through the centre of vision, it is obviously a tangent to the points which have analogous relations to that centre. The local signs or tensions of the points in such a tangent

vary in an unseizable progression; there is violence in keeping
to it, and the effect is forced. This makes the dry and stiff
quality of any long straight line, which the skilful Greeks avoided
by the curves of their columns and entablatures, and the less
economical barbarians by a profusion of interruptions and ornaments.

The straight line, when made the direct object of attention, is,
of course, followed by the eye and not seen by the outlying
parts of the retina in one eccentric position. The same explanation is good for this more common case, since the consciousness
that the eye travels in a straight line consists in the surviving
sense of the previous position, and in the manner in which the
tensions of these various positions overlap. If the tensions change
from moment to moment entirely, we have a broken, a fragmen-
tary effect, as that of zigzag, where all is dropping and picking
up again of associated motions; in the straight line, much prolonged, we have a gradual and inexorable rending of these tendencies to associated movements.

In the curves we call flowing and graceful, we have, on the
contrary, a more natural and rhythmical set of movements in the
optic muscles; and certain points in the various gyrations make
rhymes and assonances, as it were, to the eye that reaches them.
We find ourselves at every turn reawakening with a variation,
the sense of the previous position. It is easy to understand by
analogy with the superficially observed conditions of pleasure,
that such rhythms and harmonies should be delightful. The
deeper question of the physical basis of pleasure we have not
intended to discuss. Suffice it that measure, in quantity, in intensity, and in time, must involve that physiological process,
whatever it may be, the consciousness of which is pleasure.

§ 22. SYMMETRY. An important exemplification of these physiological principles is found in the charm of symmetry. When
for any reason the eye is to be habitually directed to a single
point, as to the opening of a gate or window, to an altar, a
throne, a stage, or a fireplace, there will be violence and distrac-
tion caused by the tendency to look aside in the recurring necessity of looking forward, if the object is not so arranged that the
tensions of eye are balanced, and the centre of gravity of vision
lies in the point which one is obliged to keep in sight. In all
such objects we therefore require bilateral symmetry. The necessity of vertical symmetry is not felt because the eyes and head do
not so readily survey objects from top to bottom as from side to

side. The inequality of the upper and lower parts does not generate the same tendency to motion, the same restlessness, as does the inequality of the right and left sides of an object in front of us. The comfort and economy that comes from muscular balance in the eye, is therefore in some cases the source of the value of symmetry.[1]

In other cases symmetry appeals to us through the charm of recognition and rhythm. When the eye runs over a façade, and finds the objects that attract it at equal intervals, an expectation, like the anticipation of an inevitable note or requisite word, arises in the mind, and its non-satisfaction involves a shock. This shock, if caused by the emphatic emergence of an interesting object, gives the effect of the picturesque; but when it comes with no compensation, it gives us the feeling of ugliness and imperfection—the defect which symmetry avoids. This kind of symmetry is accordingly in itself a negative merit, but often the condition of the greatest of all merits,—the permanent power to please. It contributes to that completeness which delights without stimulating, and to which our jaded senses return gladly, after all sorts of extravagances, as to a kind of domestic peace. The inwardness and solidity of this quiet beauty comes from the intrinsic character of the pleasure which makes it up. It is no adventitious charm; but the eye in its continual passage over the object finds always the same response, the same adequacy; and the very process of perception is made delightful by the object's fitness to be perceived. The parts, thus coalescing, form a single object, the unity and simplicity of which are based upon the rhythm and correspondence of its elements.

Symmetry is here what metaphysicians call a principle of individuation. By the emphasis which it lays upon the recurring elements, it cuts up the field into determinate units; all that lies between the beats is one interval, one individual. If there were no recurrent impressions, no corresponding points, the field of perception would remain a fluid continuum, without defined and recognizable divisions. The outlines of most things are symmetrical because we choose what symmetrical lines we find to be the boundaries of objects. Their symmetry is the condition of their unity, and their unity of their individuality and separate existence.

[1] The relation to stability also makes us sensitive to certain kinds of symmetry; but this is an adventitious consideration with which we are not concerned.

Experience, to be sure, can teach us to regard unsymmetrical objects as wholes, because their elements move and change together in nature; but this is a principle of individuation, *a posteriori*, founded on the association of recognized elements. These elements, to be recognized and seen to go together and form one thing, must first be somehow discriminated; and the symmetry, either of their parts, or of their position as wholes, may enable us to fix their boundaries and to observe their number. The category of unity, which we are so constantly imposing upon nature and its parts, has symmetry, then, for one of its instruments, for one of its bases of application.

If symmetry, then, is a principle of individuation and helps us to distinguish objects, we cannot wonder that it helps us to enjoy the perception. For our intelligence loves to perceive; water is not more grateful to a parched throat than a principle of comprehension to a confused understanding. Symmetry clarifies, and we all know that light is sweet. At the same time, we can see why there are limits to the value of symmetry. In objects, for instance, that are too small or too diffused for composition, symmetry has no value. In an avenue symmetry is stately and impressive, but in a large park, or in the plan of a city, or the side wall of a gallery it produces monotony in the various views rather than unity in any one of them. Greek temples, never being very large, were symmetrical on all their façades; Gothic churches were generally designed to be symmetrical only in the west front, and in the transepts, while the side elevation as a whole was eccentric. This was probably an accident, due to the demands of the interior arrangement; but it was a fortunate one, as we may see by contrasting its effect with that of our stations, exhibition buildings, and other vast structures, where symmetry is generally introduced even in the most extensive façades which, being too much prolonged for their height, cannot be treated as units. The eye is not able to take them in at a glance, and does not get the effect of repose from the balance of the extremes, while the mechanical sameness of the sections, surveyed in succession, makes the impression of an unmeaning poverty of resource.

Symmetry thus loses its value when it cannot, on account of the size of the object, contribute to the unity of our perception. The synthesis which it facilitates must be instantaneous. If the comprehension by which we unify our object is discursive, as, for instance, in conceiving the arrangement and numbering of the streets of New York, or the plan of the Escurial, the advantage of symmetry is an intellectual one; we can better imagine the relations of the parts, and draw a map of the whole in the fancy; but there is no advantage to direct perception, and therefore no added beauty. Symmetry is superfluous in those objects. Similarly animal and vegetable forms gain nothing by being symmetrically displayed, if the sense of their life and motion is to be given. When, however, these forms are used for mere decoration, not for the expression of their own vitality, then symmetry is again required to accentuate their unity and organization. This justifies the habit of conventionalizing natural forms, and the tendency of some kinds of hieratic art, like the Byzantine or Egyptian, to affect a rigid symmetry of posture. We can thereby increase the unity and force of the image without suggesting that individual life and mobility, which would interfere with the religious function of the object, as the symbol and embodiment of an impersonal faith.

§ 23. FORM THE UNITY OF A MANIFOLD. Symmetry is evidently a kind of unity in variety, where a whole is determined by the rhythmic repetition of similars. We have seen that it has a value where it is an aid to unification. Unity would thus appear to be the virtue of forms; but a moment's reflection will show us that unity cannot be absolute and be a form; a form is an aggregation, it must have elements, and the manner in which the elements are combined constitutes the character of the form. A perfectly simple perception, in which there was no consciousness of the distinction and relation of parts, would not be a perception of form; it would be a sensation. Physiologically these sensations may be aggregates and their values, as in the case of musical tones, may differ according to the manner in which certain elements, beats, vibrations, nervous processes, or what not, are combined; but for consciousness the result is simple, and the value is the pleasantness of a datum and not of a process. Form, therefore, does not appeal to the unattentive; they get from objects only a vague sensation which may in them awaken extrinsic associations; they do not stop to survey the parts or to appreciate their relation, and consequently are insensible to the various charms of various unifications; they can find in objects only the value of material or of function, not that of form.

Beauty of form, however, is what specifically appeals to an æsthetic nature; it is equally removed from the crudity of formless stimulation and from the emotional looseness of reverie and discursive thought. The indulgence in sentiment and suggestion, of which our time is fond, to the sacrifice of formal beauty, marks an absence of cultivation as real, if not as confessed, as that of the barbarian who revels in gorgeous confusion.

The synthesis, then, which constitutes form is an activity of the mind; the unity arises consciously, and is an insight into the relation of sensible elements separately perceived. It differs from sensation in the consciousness of the synthesis, and from expression in the homogeneity of the elements, and in their common presence to sense.

The variety of forms depends upon the character of the elements and on the variety of possible methods of unification. The elements may be all alike, and their only diversity be numerical. Their unity will then be merely the sense of their uniformity.[1] Or they may differ in kind, but so as to compel the mind to no particular order in their unification. Or they may finally be so constituted that they suggest inevitably the scheme of their unity; in this case there is organization in the object, and the synthesis of its parts is one and pre-determinate. We shall discuss these various forms in succession, pointing out the effects proper to each.

§ 24. MULTIPLICITY IN UNIFORMITY. The radical and typical case of the first kind of unity in variety is found in the perception of extension itself. This perception, if we look to its origin, may turn out to be primitive; no doubt the feeling of "crude extensity" is an original sensation; every inference, association, and distinction is a thing that looms up suddenly before the mind, and the nature and actuality of which is a datum of what—to indicate its irresistible immediacy and indescribability—we may well call sense. Forms are seen, and if we think of the origin of the perception, we may well call this vision a sensation. The distinction between a sensation of form, however, and one which is formless, regards the content and character, not the genesis of the perception. A distinction and association, or an inference, is a direct experience, a sensible fact; but it is the experience of a process, of a motion between two terms, and a consciousness of their coexistence and distinction; it is a feeling of relation. Now the sense of space is a feeling of this kind; the essence of it is the realization of a

[1] Cf. Fechner, *Vorschule der Aesthetik*, Erster Theil, S. 73, a passage by which the following classification of forms was first suggested.

variety of directions and of possible motions, by which the relation of point to point is vaguely but inevitably given. The perception of extension is therefore a perception of form, although of the most rudimentary kind. It is merely *Auseinandersein*, and we might call it the *materia prima* of form, were it not capable of existing without further determination. For we can have the sense of space without the sense of boundaries; indeed, this intuition is what tempts us to declare space infinite. Space would have to consist of a finite number of juxtaposed blocks, if our experience of extension carried with it essentially the realization of limits.

The æsthetic effect of extensiveness is also entirely different from that of particular shapes. Some things appeal to us by their surfaces, others by the lines that limit those surfaces. And this effect of surface is not necessarily an effect of material or colour; the evenness, monotony, and vastness of a great curtain of colour produce an effect which is that of the extreme of uniformity in the extreme of multiplicity; the eye wanders over a fluid infinity of unrecognizable positions, and the sense of their numberlessness and continuity is precisely the source of the emotion of extent. The emotion is primary and has undoubtedly a physiological ground, while the idea of size is secondary and involves associations and inferences. A small photograph of St. Peter's gives the idea of size; as does a distant view of the same object. But this is of course dependent on our realization of the distance, or of the scale of the representation. The value of size becomes immediate only when we are at close quarters with the object; then the surfaces really subtend a large angle in the field of vision, and the sense of vastness establishes its standard, which can afterwards be applied to other objects by analogy and contrast. There is also, to be sure, a moral and practical import in the known size of objects, which, by association, determines their dignity; but the pure sense of extension, based upon the attack of the object upon the apperceptive resources of the eye, is the truly æsthetic value which it concerns us to point out here, as the most rudimentary example of form.

Although the effect of extension is not that of material, the two are best seen in conjunction. Material must appear in some form; but when its beauty is to be made prominent, it is well that this form should attract attention as little as possible to itself. Now, of all forms, absolute uniformity in extension is the simplest and most allied to the material; it gives the latter only just enough form to make it real and perceptible. Very rich and beautiful materials therefore do well to assume this form. You will spoil the beauty you have by superimposing another; as if you make a statue of gold, or flute a jasper column, or bedeck a velvet cloak. The beauty of stuffs appears when they are plain. Even stone gives its specific quality best in great unbroken spaces of wall; the simplicity of the form emphasizes the substance. And again, the effect of extensity is never long satisfactory unless it is superinduced upon some material beauty; the dignity of great hangings would suffer if they were not of damask, but of cotton, and the vast smoothness of the sky would grow oppressive if it were not of so tender a blue.

§ 25. EXAMPLE OF THE STARS. Another beauty of the sky—the stars—offers so striking and fascinating an illustration of the effect of multiplicity in uniformity, that I am tempted to analyze it at some length. To most people, I fancy, the stars are beautiful; but if you asked why, they would be at a loss to reply, until they remembered what they had heard about astronomy, and the great size and distance and possible habitation of those orbs. The vague and illusive ideas thus aroused fall in so well with the dumb emotion we were already feeling, that we attribute this emotion to those ideas, and persuade ourselves that the power of the starry heavens lies in the suggestion of astronomical facts.

The idea of the insignificance of our earth and of the incomprehensible multiplicity of worlds is indeed immensely impressive; it may even be intensely disagreeable. There is something baffling about infinity; in its presence the sense of finite humility can never wholly banish the rebellious suspicion that we are being deluded. Our mathematical imagination is put on the rack by an attempted conception that has all the anguish of a nightmare and probably, could we but awake, all its laughable absurdity. But the obsession of this dream is an intellectual puzzle, not an æsthetic delight. It is not essential to our admiration. Before the days of Kepler the heavens declared the glory of the Lord; and we needed no calculation of stellar distances, no fancies about a plurality of worlds, no image of infinite spaces, to make the stars sublime.

Had we been taught to believe that the stars governed our fortunes, and were we reminded of fate whenever we looked at them, we should similarly tend to imagine that this belief was the source of their sublimity; and, if the superstition were dispelled, we should think the interest gone from the apparition. But experience would soon undeceive us, and prove to us that the sensuous character of the object was sublime in itself. Indeed, on account of that intrinsic sublimity the sky can be fitly chosen as a symbol for a sublime conception; the common quality in both makes each suggest the other. For that reason, too, the parable of the natal stars governing our lives is such a natural one to express our subjection to circumstances, and can be transformed by the stupidity of disciples into a literal tenet. In the same way, the kinship of the emotion produced by the stars with the emotion proper to certain religious moments makes the stars seem a religious object. They become, like impressive music, a stimulus to worship. But fortunately there are experiences which remain untouched by theory, and which maintain the mutual intelligence of men through the estrangements wrought by intellectual and religious systems. When the superstructures crumble, the common foundation of human sentience and imagination is exposed beneath.

The intellectual suggestion of the infinity of nature can, moreover, be awakened by other experiences which are by no means sublime. A heap of sand will involve infinity as surely as a universe of suns and planets. Any object is infinitely divisible and, when we press the thought, can contain as many worlds with as many winged monsters and ideal republics as can the satellites of Sirius. But the infinitesimal does not move us æsthetically; it can only awaken an amused curiosity. The difference cannot lie in the import of the idea, which is objectively the same in both cases. It lies in the different immediate effect of the crude images which give us the type and meaning of each; the crude image that underlies the idea of the infinitesimal is the dot, the poorest and most uninteresting of impressions; while the crude image that underlies the idea of infinity is space, multiplicity in uniformity, and this, as we have seen, has a powerful effect on account of the breadth, volume, and omnipresence of the stimulation. Every point in the retina is evenly excited, and the local signs of all are simultaneously felt. This equable tension, this balance and elasticity in the very absence of fixity, give the vague but powerful feeling that we wish to describe. Did not the infinite, by this initial assault upon our senses, awe us and overwhelm us, as solemn music might, the idea of it would be abstract and moral like that of the infinitesimal, and nothing but an amusing curiosity.

Nothing is objectively impressive; things are impressive only when they succeed in touching the sensibility of the observer, by finding the avenues to his brain and heart. The idea that the universe is a multitude of minute spheres circling, like specks of dust, in a dark and boundless void, might leave us cold and in-different, if not bored and depressed, were it not that we identify this hypothetical scheme with the visible splendour, the poignant intensity, and the baffling number of the stars. So far is the object from giving value to the impression, that it is here, as it must always ultimately be, the impression that gives value to the object. For all worth leads us back to actual feeling some-where, or else evaporates into nothing—into a word and a super-stition.

Now, the starry heavens are very happily designed to intensify the sensations on which their beauties must rest. In the first place, the continuum of space is broken into points, numerous enough to give the utmost idea of multiplicity, and yet so dis-tinct and vivid that it is impossible not to remain aware of their individuality. The variety of local signs, without becoming organized into forms, remains prominent and irreducible. This makes the object infinitely more exciting than a plane surface would be. In the second place, the sensuous contrast of the dark background,—blacker the clearer the night and the more stars we can see,—with the palpitating fire of the stars themselves, could not be exceeded by any possible device. This material beauty adds incalculably, as we have already pointed out, to the inwardness and sublimity of the effect. To realize the great im-portance of these two elements, we need but to conceive their absence, and observe the change in the dignity of the result.

Fancy a map of the heavens and every star plotted upon it, even those invisible to the naked eye: why would this object, as full of scientific suggestion surely as the reality, leave us so comparatively cold? Quite indifferent it might not leave us, for I have myself watched stellar photographs with almost inexhaust-ible wonder. The sense of multiplicity is naturally in no way diminished by the representation; but the poignancy of the sensation, the life of the light, are gone; and with the dulled impression the keenness of the emotion disappears. Or imagine the stars, undiminished in number, without losing any of their astronomical significance and divine immutability, marshalled in geometrical patterns; say in a Latin cross, with the words *In hoc signo vinces* in a scroll around them. The beauty of the il-lumination would be perhaps increased, and its import, practical, religious, and cosmic, would surely be a little plainer; but where would be the sublimity of the spectacle? Irretrievably lost: and lost because the form of the object would no longer tantalize us with its sheer multiplicity, and with the consequent over-powering sense of suspense and awe.

In a word, the infinity which moves us is the sense of multi-plicity in uniformity. Accordingly things which have enough multiplicity, as the lights of a city seen across water, have an effect similar to that of the stars, if less intense; whereas a star, if alone, because the multiplicity is lacking, makes a wholly dif-ferent impression. The single star is tender, beautiful, and mild; we can compare it to the humblest and sweetest of things:

> A violet by a mossy stone
> Half hidden from the eye,
> Fair as *a star when only one*
> *Is shining in the sky.*

It is, not only in fact but in nature, an attendant on the moon, associated with the moon, if we may be so prosaic here, not only by contiguity but also by similarity.

> Fairer than Phœbe's sapphire-regioned star
> Or vesper, amorous glow-worm of the sky.

The same poet can say elsewhere of a passionate lover:

> He arose
> Ethereal, flushed, and like a throbbing star,
> Amid the sapphire heaven's deep repose.

How opposite is all this from the cold glitter, the cruel and mysterious sublimity of the stars when they are many! With these we have no Sapphic associations; they make us think rather of Kant who could hit on nothing else to compare with his cate-gorical imperative, perhaps because he found in both the same baffling incomprehensibility and the same fierce actuality. Such ultimate feelings are sensations of physical tension.

§ 26. DEFECTS OF PURE MULTIPLICITY. This long analysis will be a sufficient illustration of the power of multiplicity in uni-formity; we may now proceed to point out the limitations in-herent in this form. The most obvious one is that of monotony; a file of soldiers or an iron railing is impressive in its way, but cannot long entertain us, nor hold us with that depth of develop-ing interest, with which we might study a crowd or a forest of trees.

The tendency of monotony is double, and in two directions deadens our pleasure. When the repeated impressions are acute, and cannot be forgotten in their endless repetition, their monotony becomes painful. The constant appeal to the same sense, the constant requirement of the same reaction, tires the system, and we long for change as for a relief. If the repeated stimulations are not very acute, we soon become unconscious of them; like the ticking of the clock, they become merely a factor in our bodily tone, a cause, as the case may be, of a diffused pleasure or unrest; but they cease to present a distinguishable object.

The pleasures, therefore, which a kindly but monotonous environment produces, often fail to make it beautiful, for the simple reason that the environment is not perceived. Likewise the hideousness of things to which we are accustomed—the blemishes of the landscape, the ugliness of our clothes or of our walls—does not oppress us, not so much because we do not see the ugliness as because we overlook the things. The beauties or defects of monotonous objects are easily lost, because the objects are themselves intermittent in consciousness. But it is of some practical importance to remark that this indifference of monotonous values is more apparent than real. The particular object ceases to be of consequence; but the congruity of its structure and quality with our faculties of perception remains, and its presence in our environment is still a constant source of vague irritation and friction, or of subtle and pervasive delight. And this value, although not associated with the image of the monotonous object, lies there in our mind, like all the vital and systemic feelings, ready to enhance the beauty of any object that arouses our attention, and meantime adding to the health and freedom of our life—making whatever we do a little easier and pleasanter for us. A grateful environment is a substitute for happiness. It can quicken us from without as a fixed hope and affection, or the consciousness of a right life, can quicken us from within. To humanize our surroundings is, therefore, a task which should interest the physicians both of soul and body.

But the monotony of multiplicity is not merely intrinsic in the form; what is perhaps even of greater consequence in the arts is the fact that its capacity for association is restricted. What is in itself uniform cannot have a great diversity of relations. Hence the dryness, the crisp definiteness and hardness, of those products of art which contain an endless repetition of the same elements. Their affinities are necessarily few; they are not fit for many uses, nor capable of expressing many ideas. The heroic couplet, now too much derided, is a form of this kind. Its compactness and inevitableness make it excellent for an epigram and adequate it for a satire, but its perpetual snap and unvarying rhythm are thin for an epic, and impossible for a song. The Greek colonnade, a form in many ways analogous, has similar limitations. Beautiful with a finished and restrained beauty, which our taste is hardly refined enough to appreciate, it is incapable of development. The experiments of Roman architecture sufficiently show it; the glory of which is their Roman frame rather than their Hellenic ornament.

When the Greeks themselves had to face the problem of larger and more complex buildings, in the service of a supernatural and hierarchical system, they transformed their architecture into what we call Byzantine, and St. Sophia took the place of the Parthenon. Here a vast vault was introduced, the colonnade disappeared, the architrave was rounded into an arch from column to column, the capitals of these were changed from concave to convex, and a thousand other changes in structure and ornament introduced flexibility and variety. Architecture could in this way, precisely because more vague and barbarous, better adapt itself to the conditions of the new epoch. Perfect taste is itself a limitation, not because it intentionally excludes any excellence, but because it impedes the wandering of the arts into those bypaths of caprice and grotesqueness in which, although at the sacrifice of formal beauty, interesting partial effects might still be discovered. And this objection applies with double force to the first crystallizations of taste, when tradition has carried us but a little way in the right direction. The authorized effects are then very simple, and if we allow no others, our art becomes wholly inadequate to the functions ultimately imposed upon it. Primitive arts might furnish examples, but the state of English poetry at the time of Queen Anne is a sufficient illustration of this possibility. The French classicism, of which the English school was an echo, was more vital and human, because it embodied a more native taste and a wider training.

§ 27. ÆSTHETICS OF DEMOCRACY. It would be an error to suppose that æsthetic principles apply only to our judgments of works of art or of those natural objects which we attend to chiefly on account of their beauty. Every idea which is formed in the human mind, every activity and emotion, has some relation, direct or indirect, to pain and pleasure. If, as is the case in all the more important instances, these fluid activities and emotions precipitate, as it were, in their evanescence certain psychical solids called ideas of things, then the concomitant pleasures are incorporated more or less in those concrete ideas and the things acquire an æsthetic colouring. And although this æsthetic colour-ing may be the last quality we notice in objects of practical interest, its influence upon us is none the less real, and often accounts for a great deal in our moral and practical attitude.

In the leading political and moral idea of our time, in the idea of democracy, I think there is a strong æsthetic ingredient, and the power of the idea of democracy over the imagination is an illustration of that effect of multiplicity in uniformity which we have been studying. Of course, nothing could be more absurd than to suggest that the French Revolution, with its immense im-plications, had an æsthetic preference for its basis; it sprang, as we know, from the hatred of oppression, the rivalry of classes, and the aspiration after a freer social and strictly moral organiza-tion. But when these moral forces were suggesting and partly realizing the democratic idea, this idea was necessarily vividly present to men's thoughts; the picture of human life which it presented was becoming familiar, and was being made the sanc-tion and goal of constant endeavour. Nothing so much enhances a good as to make sacrifices for it. The consequence was that democracy, prized at first as a means to happiness and as an in-strument of good government, was acquiring an intrinsic value; it was beginning to seem good in itself, in fact, the only intrin-sically right and perfect arrangement. A utilitarian scheme was receiving an æsthetic consecration. That which was happening to democracy had happened before to the feudal and royalist systems; they too had come to be prized in themselves, for the pleasure men took in thinking of society organized in such an ancient, and thereby to their fancy, appropriate and beautiful manner. The practical value of the arrangement, on which, of course, it is entirely dependent for its origin and authority, was forgotten, and men were ready to sacrifice their welfare to their sense of propriety; that is, they allowed an æsthetic good to out-weigh a practical one. That seems now a superstition, although, indeed, a very natural and even noble one. Equally natural and noble, but no less superstitious, is our own belief in the divine right of democracy. Its essential right is something purely æsthetic.

Such æsthetic love of uniformity, however, is usually disguised under some moral label: we call it the love of justice, perhaps because we have not considered that the value of justice also, in so far as it is not derivative and utilitarian, must be intrinsic, or, what is practically the same thing, æsthetic. But occasionally the beauties of democracy are presented to us undisguised. The

writings of Walt Whitman are a notable example. Never, perhaps, has the charm of uniformity in multiplicity been felt so
completely and so exclusively. Everywhere it greets us with a
passionate preference; not flowers but leaves of grass, not music
but drum-taps, not composition but aggregation, not the hero
but the average man, not the crisis but the vulgarest moment; and
by this resolute marshalling of nullities, by this effort to show
us everything as a momentary pulsation of a liquid and structure-
less whole, he profoundly stirs the imagination. We may wish to
dislike this power, but, I think, we must inwardly admire it. For
whatever practical dangers we may see in this terrible levelling,
our æsthetic faculty can condemn no actual effect; its privilege is
to be pleased by opposites, and to be capable of finding chaos
sublime without ceasing to make nature beautiful.

§ 28. VALUES OF TYPES AND VALUES OF EXAMPLES. It is time we
should return to the consideration of abstract forms. Nearest in
nature to the example of uniformity in multiplicity, we found
those objects, like a reversible pattern, that having some variety
of parts invite us to survey them in different orders, and so bring
into play in a marked manner the faculty of apperception.

There is in the senses, as we have seen, a certain form of stimulation, a certain measure and rhythm of waves with which the
æsthetic value of the sensation is connected. So when, in the
perception of the object, a notable contribution is made by
memory and mental habit, the value of the perception will be
due, not only to the pleasantness of the external stimulus, but
also to the pleasantness of the apperceptive reaction; and the
latter source of value will be more important in proportion as the
object perceived is more dependent, for the form and meaning
it presents, upon our past experience and imaginative trend, and
less on the structure of the external object.

Our apperception of form varies not only with our constitution, age, and health, as does the appreciation of sensuous values,
but also with our education and genius. The more indeterminate
the object, the greater share must subjective forces have in determining our perception; for, of course, every perception is in itself
perfectly specific, and can be called indefinite only in reference to
an abstract ideal which it is expected to approach. Every cloud
has just the outline it has, although we may call it vague, because we cannot classify its form under any geometrical or animal
species; it would be first definitely a whale, and then would become indefinite until we saw our way to calling it a camel. But

while in the intermediate stage, the cloud would be a form in the perception of which there would be little apperceptive activity, little reaction from the store of our experience, little sense of form; its value would be in its colour and transparency, and in the suggestion of lightness and of complex but gentle movement.

But the moment we said "Yes, very like a whale," a new kind of value would appear; the cloud could now be beautiful or ugly, not as a cloud merely, but as a whale. We do not speak now of the associations of the idea, as with the sea, or fishermen's yarns; that is an extrinsic matter of expression. We speak simply of the intrinsic value of the form of the whale, of its lines, its movement, its proportion. This is a more or less individual set of images which are revived in the act of recognition; this revival constitutes the recognition, and the beauty of the form is the pleasure of that revival. A certain musical phrase, as it were, is played in the brain; the awakening of that echo is the act of apperception and the harmony of the present stimulation with the form of that phrase; the power of this particular object to develope and intensify that generic phrase in the direction of pleasure, is the test of the formal beauty of this example. For these cerebral phrases have a certain rhythm; this rhythm can, by the influence of the stimulus that now reawakens it, be marred or enriched, be made more or less marked and delicate; and as this conflict or reinforcement comes, the object is ugly or beautiful in form.

Such an æsthetic value is thus dependent on two things. The first is the acquired character of the apperceptive form evoked; it may be a cadenza or a trill, a major or a minor chord, a rose or a violet, a goddess or a dairy-maid; and as one or another of these is recognized, an æsthetic dignity and tone is given to the object. But it will be noticed that in such mere recognition very little pleasure is found, or, what is the same thing, different æsthetic types in the abstract have little difference in intrinsic beauty. The great difference lies in their affinities. What will decide us to like or not to like the type of our apperception will be not so much what this type is, as its fitness to the context of our mind. It is like a word in a poem, more effective by its fitness than by its intrinsic beauty, although that is requisite too. We can be shocked at an incongruity of natures more than we can be pleased by the intrinsic beauty of each nature apart, so long, that is, as they remain abstract natures, objects recognized without being studied. The æsthetic dignity of the form, then, tells us the kind of beauty we are to expect, affects us by its welcome or unwelcome promise, but hardly gives us a positive pleasure in the beauty itself.

Now this is the first thing in the value of a form, the value of the type as such; the second and more important element is the relation of the particular impression to the form under which it is apperceived. This determines the value of the object as an example of its class. After our mind is pitched to the key and rhythm of a certain idea, say of a queen, it remains for the impression to fulfil, aggrandize, or enrich this form by a sympathetic embodiment of it. Then we have a queen that is truly royal. But if instead there is disappointment, if this particular queen is an ugly one, although perhaps she might have pleased as a witch, this is because the apperceptive form and the impression give a cerebral discord. The object is unideal, that is, the novel, external element is inharmonious with the revived and internal element by suggesting which the object has been apperceived.

§ 29. Origin of types. A most important thing, therefore, in the perception of form is the formation of types in our mind, with reference to which examples are to be judged. I say the formation of them, for we can hardly consider the theory that they are eternal as a possible one in psychology. The Platonic doctrine on that point is a striking illustration of an equivocation we mentioned in the beginning;[1] namely, that the import of an experience is regarded as a manifestation of its cause—the product of a faculty substituted for the description of its function. Eternal types are the instrument of æsthetic life, not its foundation. Take the æsthetic attitude, and you have for the moment an eternal idea; an idea, I mean, that you treat as an absolute standard, just as when you take the perceptive attitude you have an external object which you treat as an absolute existence. But the æsthetic, like the perceptive faculty, can be made an object of study in turn, and its theory can be sought; and then the eternal idea, like the external object, is seen to be a product of human nature, a symbol of experience, and an instrument of thought.

The question whether there are not, in external nature or in the mind of God, objects and eternal types, is indeed not settled, it is not even touched by this inquiry; but it is indirectly shown to be futile, because such transcendent realities, if they exist,

1 See Introduction, p. 9.

can have nothing to do with our ideas of them. The Platonic idea of a tree may exist; how should I deny it? How should I deny that I might some day find myself outside the sky gazing at it, and feeling that I, with my mental vision, am beholding the plenitude of arboreal beauty, perceived in this world only as a vague essence haunting the multiplicity of finite trees? But what can that have to do with my actual sense of what a tree should be? Shall we take the Platonic myth literally, and say the idea is a memory of the tree I have already seen in heaven? How else establish any relation between that eternal object and the type in my mind? But why, in that case, this infinite variability of ideal trees? Was the Tree Beautiful an oak, or a cedar, an English or an American elm? My actual types are finite and mutually exclusive; that heavenly type must be one and infinite. The problem is hopeless.

Very simple, on the other hand, is the explanation of the existence of that type as a residuum of experience. Our idea of an individual thing is a compound and residuum of our several experiences of it; and in the same manner our idea of a class is a compound and residuum of our ideas of the particulars that compose it. Particular impressions have, by virtue of their intrinsic similarity or of the identity of their relations, a tendency to be merged and identified, so that many individual perceptions leave but a single blurred memory that stands for them all, because it combines their several associations. Similarly, when various objects have many common characteristics, the mind is incapable of keeping them apart. It cannot hold clearly so great a multitude of distinctions and relations as would be involved in naming and conceiving separately each grain of sand, or drop of water, each fly or horse or man that we have ever seen. The mass of our experience has therefore to be classified, if it is to be available at all. Instead of a distinct image to represent each of our original impressions, we have a general resultant—a composite photograph—of those impressions.

This resultant image is the idea of the class. It often has very few, if any, of the sensible properties of the particulars that underlie it, often an artificial symbol—the sound of a word—is the only element, present to all the instances, which the generic image clearly contains. For, of course, the reason why a name can represent a class of objects is that the name is the most conspicuous element of identity in the various experiences of objects in that class. We have seen many horses, but if we are not lovers of the animal, nor particularly keen observers, very likely we retain no clear image of all that mass of impressions except the reverberation of the sound "horse," which really or mentally has accompanied all those impressions. This sound, therefore, is the content of our general idea, and to it cling all the associations which constitute our sense of what the word means. But a person with a memory predominantly visual would probably add to this remembered sound a more or less detailed image of the animal; some particular horse in some particular attitude might possibly be recalled, but more probably some imaginative construction, some dream image, would accompany the sound. An image which reproduced no particular horse exactly, but which was a spontaneous fiction of the fancy, would serve, by virtue of its felt relations, the same purpose as the sound itself. Such a spontaneous image would be, of course, variable. In fact, no image can, strictly speaking, ever recur. But these percepts, as they are called, springing up in the mind like flowers from the buried seeds of past experience, would inherit all the powers of suggestion which are required by any instrument of classification.

These powers of suggestion have probably a cerebral basis. The new percept—the generic idea—repeats to a great extent, both in nature and localization, the excitement constituting the various original impressions; as the percept reproduces more or less of these it will be a more or less full and impartial representative of them. Not all the suggestions of a word or image are equally ripe. A generic idea or type usually presents to us a very inadequate and biassed view of the field it means to cover. As we reflect and seek to correct this inadequacy, the percept changes on our hands. The very consciousness that other individuals and other qualities fall under our concept, changes this concept, as a psychological presence, and alters its distinctness and extent. When I remember, to use a classical example, that the triangle is not isosceles, nor scalene, nor rectangular, but each and all of those, I reduce my percept to the word and its definition, with perhaps a sense of the general motion of the hand and eye by which we trace a three-cornered figure.

Since the production of a general idea is thus a matter of subjective bias, we cannot expect that a type should be the exact average of the examples from which it is drawn. In a rough way, it is the average; a fact that in itself is the strongest of arguments against the independence or priority of the general idea. The beautiful horse, the beautiful speech, the beautiful face, is always a medium between the extremes which our experience has offered. It is enough that a given characteristic should be generally present in our experience, for it to become an indispensable element of the ideal. There is nothing in itself beautiful or necessary in the shape of the human ear, or in the presence of nails on the fingers and toes; but the ideal of man, which the preposterous conceit of our judgment makes us set up as divine and eternal, requires these precise details; without them the human form would be repulsively ugly.

It often happens that the accidents of experience make us in this way introduce into the ideal, elements which, if they could be excluded without disgusting us, would make possible satisfactions greater than those we can now enjoy. Thus the taste formed by one school of art may condemn the greater beauties created by another. In morals we have the same phenomenon. A barbarous ideal of life requires tasks and dangers incompatible with happiness; a rude and oppressed conscience is incapable of regarding as good a state which excludes its own acrid satisfactions. So, too, a fanatical imagination cannot regard God as just unless he is represented as infinitely cruel. The purpose of education is, of course, to free us from these prejudices, and to develope our ideals in the direction of the greatest possible good. Evidently the ideal has been formed by the habit of perception; it is, in a rough way, that average form which we expect and most readily apperceive. The propriety and necessity of it is entirely relative to our experience and faculty of apperception. The shock of surprise, the incongruity with the formed percept, is the essence and measure of ugliness.

§ 30. The average modified in the direction of pleasure. Nevertheless we do not form æsthetic ideals any more than other general types, entirely without bias. We have already observed that a percept seldom gives an impartial compound of the objects of which it is the generic image. This partiality is due to a variety of circumstances. One is the unequal accuracy of our observation. If some interest directs our attention to a particular quality of objects, that quality will be prominent in our percept; it may even be the only content clearly given in our general idea; and any object, however similar in other respects to those of the given class, will at once be distinguished as belonging to a different species if it lacks that characteristic on which our attention is particularly fixed. Our percepts are thus habitually biassed in the direction of practical interest, if practical interest does not indeed entirely govern their formation. In the same manner, our æsthetic ideals are biassed in the direction of æsthetic interest. Not all parts of an object are equally congruous with our perceptive faculty; not all elements are noted with the same pleasure. Those, therefore, which are agreeable are chiefly dwelt upon by the lover of beauty, and his percept will give an average of things with a great emphasis laid on that part of them which is beautiful. The ideal will thus deviate from the average in the direction of the observer's pleasure.

For this reason the world is so much more beautiful to a poet or an artist than to an ordinary man. Each object, as his æsthetic sense is developed, is perhaps less beautiful than to the uncritical eye; his taste becomes difficult, and only the very best gives him unalloyed satisfaction. But while each work of nature and art is thus apparently blighted by his greater demands and keener susceptibility, the world itself, and the various natures it contains, are to him unspeakably beautiful. The more blemishes he can see in men, the more excellence he sees in man, and the more bitterly he laments the fate of each particular soul, the more reverence and love he has for the soul in its ideal essence. Criticism and idealization involve each other. The habit of looking for beauty in everything makes us notice the shortcomings of things; our sense, hungry for complete satisfaction, misses the perfection it demands. But this demand for perfection becomes at the same time the nucleus of our observation; from every side a quick affinity draws what is beautiful together and stores it in the mind, giving body there to the blind yearnings of our nature. Many imperfect things crystallize into a single perfection. The mind is thus peopled by general ideas in which beauty is the chief quality; and these ideas are at the same time the types of things. The type is still a natural resultant of particular impressions; but the formation of it has been guided by a deep subjective bias in favour of what has delighted the eye.

This theory can be easily tested by asking whether, in the case where the ideal differs from the average form of objects, this variation is not due to the intrinsic pleasantness or impressiveness of the quality exaggerated. For instance, in the human form, the ideal differs immensely from the average. In many respects the extreme or something near it is the most beautiful. Xenophon describes the women of Armenia as καλλαὶ καί μεγάλαι, and we should still speak of one as fair and tall and of another as fair but little. Size is therefore, even where least requisite, a thing in which the ideal exceeds the average. And the reason—apart from associations of strength—is that unusual size makes things conspicuous. The first prerequisite of effect is impression, and size helps that; therefore in the æsthetic ideal the average will be modified by being enlarged, because that is a change in the direction of our pleasure, and size will be an element of beauty.[1]

Similarly the eyes, in themselves beautiful, will be enlarged also; and generally whatever makes by its sensuous quality, by its abstract form, or by its expression, a particular appeal to our attention and contribution to our delight, will count for more in the ideal type than its frequency would warrant. The generic image has been constructed under the influence of a selective attention, bent upon æsthetic worth.

To praise any object for approaching the ideal of its kind is therefore only a roundabout way of specifying its intrinsic merit and expressing its direct effect on our sensibility. If in referring to the ideal we were not thus analyzing the real, the ideal would be an irrelevant and unmeaning thing. We know what the ideal is because we observe what pleases us in the reality. If we allow the general notion to tyrannize at all over the particular impression and to blind us to new and unclassified beauties which the latter may contain, we are simply substituting words for feelings, and making a verbal classification pass for an æsthetic judgment. Then the sense of beauty is gone to seed. Ideals have their uses, but their authority is wholly representative. They stand for specific satisfactions, or else they stand for nothing at all.

In fact, the whole machinery of our intelligence, our general ideas and laws, fixed and external objects, principles, persons, and gods, are so many symbolic, algebraic expressions. They stand for experience; experience which we are incapable of retaining and surveying in its multitudinous immediacy. We should flounder hopelessly, like the animals, did we not keep ourselves afloat and direct our course by these intellectual devices. Theory helps us to bear our ignorance of fact.

The same thing happens, in a way, in other fields. Our armies are devices necessitated by our weakness; our property an encumbrance required by our need. If our situation were not precarious, these great engines of death and life would not be invented. And our intelligence is such another weapon against fate. We need not lament the fact, since, after all, to build these

---

[1] The contention of Burke that the beautiful is small is due to an arbitrary definition. By beautiful he means pretty and charming; agreeable as opposed to impressive. He only exaggerates the then usual opposition of the beautiful to the sublime.

various structures is, up to a certain point, the natural function of human nature. The trouble is not that the products are always subjective, but that they are sometimes unfit and torment the spirit which they exercise. The pathetic part of our situation appears only when we so attach ourselves to those necessary but imperfect fictions, as to reject the facts from which they spring and of which they seek to be prophetic. We are then guilty of that substitution of means for ends, which is called idolatry in religion, absurdity in logic, and folly in morals. In æsthetics the thing has no name, but is nevertheless very common; for it is found whenever we speak of what ought to please, rather than of what actually pleases.

§ 31. ARE ALL THINGS BEAUTIFUL? These principles lead to an intelligible answer to a question which is not uninteresting in itself and crucial in a system of æsthetics. Are all things beautiful? Are all types equally beautiful when we abstract from our practical prejudices? If the reader has given his assent to the foregoing propositions, he will easily see that, in one sense, we must declare that no object is essentially ugly. If impressions are painful, they are objectified with difficulty; the perception of a thing is therefore, under normal circumstances, when the senses are not fatigued, rather agreeable than disagreeable. And when the frequent perception of a class of objects has given rise to an apperceptive norm, and we have an ideal of the species, the recognition and exemplification of that norm will give pleasure, in proportion to the degree of interest and accuracy with which we have made our observations. The naturalist accordingly sees beauties to which the academic artist is blind, and each new environment must open to us, if we allow it to educate our perception, a new wealth of beautiful forms.

But we are not for this reason obliged to assert that all gradations of beauty and dignity are a matter of personal and accidental bias. The mystics who declare that to God there is no distinction in the value of things, and that only our human prejudice makes us prefer a rose to an oyster, or a lion to a monkey, have, of course, a reason for what they say. If we could strip ourselves of our human nature, we should undoubtedly find ourselves incapable of making these distinctions, as well as of thinking, perceiving, or willing in any way which is now possible to us. But how things would appear to us if we were not human is, to a man, a question of no importance. Even the mystic to whom the definite constitution of his own mind is so hateful, can only paralyze without transcending his faculties. A passionate negation, the motive of which, although morbid, is in spite of itself perfectly human, absorbs all his energies, and his ultimate triumph is to attain the absoluteness of indifference.

What is true of mysticism in general, is true also of its manifestation in æsthetics. If we could so transform our taste as to find beauty everywhere, because, perhaps, the ultimate nature of things is as truly exemplified in one thing as in another, we should, in fact, have abolished taste altogether. For the ascending series of æsthetic satisfactions we should have substituted a monotonous judgment of identity. If things are beautiful not by virtue of their differences but by virtue of an identical something which they equally contain, then there could be no discrimination in beauty. Like substance, beauty would be everywhere one and the same, and any tendency to prefer one thing to another would be a proof of finitude and illusion. When we try to make our judgments absolute, what we do is to surrender our natural standards and categories, and slip into another genus, until we lose ourselves in the satisfying vagueness of mere being.

Relativity to our partial nature is therefore essential to all our definite thoughts, judgments, and feelings. And when once the human bias is admitted as a legitimate, because for us a necessary, basis of preference, the whole wealth of nature is at once organized by that standard into a hierarchy of values. Everything is beautiful because everything is capable in some degree of interesting and charming our attention; but things differ immensely in this capacity to please us in the contemplation of them, and therefore they differ immensely in beauty. Could our nature be fixed and determined once for all in every particular, the scale of æsthetic values would become certain. We should not dispute about tastes, no longer because a common principle of preference could not be discovered, but rather because any disagreement would then be impossible.

As a matter of fact, however, human nature is a vague abstraction; that which is common to all men is the least part of their natural endowment. Æsthetic capacity is accordingly very unevenly distributed; and the world of beauty is much vaster and more complex to one man than to another. So long, indeed, as the distinction is merely one of development, so that we recognize in the greatest connoisseur only the refinement of the judgments of the rudest peasant, our æsthetic principle has not changed; we might say that, in so far, we had a common standard more or less widely applied. We might say so, because that standard would be an implication of a common nature more or less fully developed.

But men do not differ only in the degree of their susceptibility, they differ also in its direction. Human nature branches into opposed and incompatible characters. And taste follows this bifurcation. We cannot, except whimsically, say that a taste for music is higher or lower than a taste for sculpture. A man might be a musician and a sculptor by turns; that would only involve a perfectly conceivable enlargement in human genius. But the union thus effected would be an accumulation of gifts in the observer, not a combination of beauties in the object. The excellence of sculpture and that of music would remain entirely independent and heterogeneous. Such divergences are like those of the outer senses to which these arts appeal. Sound and colour have analogies only in their lowest depth, as vibrations and excitement; as they grow specific and objective, they diverge; and although the same consciousness perceives them, it perceives them as unrelated and uncombinable objects.

The ideal enlargement of human capacity, therefore, has no tendency to constitute a single standard of beauty. These standards remain the expression of diverse habits of sense and imagination. The man who combines the greatest range with the greatest endowment in each particular, will, of course, be the critic most generally respected. He will express the feelings of the greater number of men. The advantage of scope in criticism lies not in the improvement of our sense in each particular field; here the artist will detect the amateur's shortcomings. But no man is a specialist with his whole soul. Some latent capacity he has for other perceptions; and it is for the awakening of these, and their marshalling before him, that the student of each kind of beauty turns to the lover of them all.

The temptation, therefore, to say that all things are really equally beautiful arises from an imperfect analysis, by which the operations of the æsthetic consciousness are only partially disintegrated. The dependence of the *degrees* of beauty upon our nature is perceived, while the dependence of its *essence* upon our nature is still ignored. All things are not equally beautiful because the subjective bias that discriminates between them is the cause of their being beautiful at all. The principle of personal preference is the same as that of human taste; real and objective beauty, in contrast to a vagary of individuals, means only an affinity to a more prevalent and lasting susceptibility, a

response to a more general and fundamental demand. And the
keener discrimination, by which the distance between beautiful
and ugly things is increased, far from being a loss of æsthetic
insight, is a development of that faculty by the exercise of which
beauty comes into the world.

§ 32. EFFECTS OF INDETERMINATE ORGANIZATION. It is the free
exercise of the activity of apperception that gives so peculiar an
interest to indeterminate objects, to the vague, the incoherent,
the suggestive, the variously interpretable. The more this effect
is appealed to, the greater wealth of thought is presumed in the
observer, and the less mastery is displayed by the artist. A poor
and literal mind cannot enjoy the opportunity for reverie and
construction given by the stimulus of indeterminate objects; it
lacks the requisite resources. It is nonplussed and annoyed, and
turns away to simpler and more transparent things with a feeling of helplessness often turning into contempt. And, on the
other hand, the artist who is not artist enough, who has too
many irrepressible talents and too little technical skill, is sure
to float in the region of the indeterminate. He sketches and never
paints; he hints and never expresses; he stimulates and never in-
forms. This is the method of the individuals and of the nations
that have more genius than art.

The consciousness that accompanies this characteristic is the
sense of profundity, of mighty significance. And this feeling is
not necessarily an illusion. The nature of our materials—be they
words, colours, or plastic matter—imposes a limit and bias upon
our expression. The reality of experience can never be quite
rendered through these media. The greatest mastery of technique
will therefore come short of perfect adequacy and exhaustive-
ness; there must always remain a penumbra and fringe of suggestion if the most explicit representation is to communicate a
truth. When there is real profundity,—when the living core of
things is most firmly grasped,—there will accordingly be a felt
inadequacy of expression, and an appeal to the observer to piece
out our imperfections with his thoughts. But this should come
only after the resources of a patient and well-learned art have
been exhausted; else what is felt as depth is really confusion
and incompetence. The simplest thing becomes unutterable, if
we have forgotten how to speak. And a habitual indulgence in
the inarticulate is a sure sign of the philosopher who has not
learned to think, the poet who has not learned to write, the
painter who has not learned to paint, and the impression that

has not learned to express itself—all of which are compatible with an immensity of genius in the inexpressible soul.

Our age is given to this sort of self-indulgence, and on both the grounds mentioned. Our public, without being really trained, —for we appeal to too large a public to require training in it,— is well informed and eagerly responsive to everything; it is ready to work pretty hard, and do its share towards its own profit and entertainment. It becomes a point of pride with it to understand and appreciate everything. And our art, in its turn, does not overlook this opportunity. It becomes disorganized, sporadic, whimsical, and experimental. The crudity we are too distracted to refine, we accept as originality, and the vagueness we are too pretentious to make accurate, we pass off as sublimity. This is the secret of making great works on novel principles, and of writing hard books easily.

§ 33. EXAMPLE OF LANDSCAPE. An extraordinary taste for landscape compensates us for this ignorance of what is best and most finished in the arts. The natural landscape is an indeterminate object; it almost always contains enough diversity to allow the eye a great liberty in selecting, emphasizing, and grouping its elements, and it is furthermore rich in suggestion and in vague emotional stimulus. A landscape to be seen has to be composed, and to be loved has to be moralized. That is the reason why rude or vulgar people are indifferent to their natural surroundings. It does not occur to them that the work-a-day world is capable of æsthetic contemplation. Only on holidays, when they add to themselves and their belongings some unusual ornament, do they stop to watch the effect. The far more beautiful daily aspects of their environment escape them altogether. When, however, we learn to apperceive; when we grow fond of tracing lines and developing vistas; when, above all, the subtler influences of places on our mental tone are transmuted into an expressiveness in those places, and they are furthermore poetized by our day-dreams, and turned by our instant fancy into so many hints of a fairyland of happy living and vague adventure,—then we feel that the landscape is beautiful. The forest, the fields, all wild or rural scenes, are then full of companionship and entertainment.

This is a beauty dependent on reverie, fancy, and objectified emotion. The promiscuous natural landscape cannot be enjoyed in any other way. It has no real unity, and therefore requires to have some form or other supplied by the fancy; which can be the more readily done, in that the possible forms are many, and the constant changes in the object offer varying suggestions to the eye. In fact, psychologically speaking, there is no such thing as a landscape; what we call such is an infinity of different scraps and glimpses given in succession. Even a painted land- scape, although it tends to select and emphasize some parts of the field, is composed by adding together a multitude of views. When this painting is observed in its turn, it is surveyed as a real landscape would be, and apperceived partially and piece- meal; although, of course, it offers much less wealth of material than its living original, and is therefore vastly inferior.

Only the extreme of what is called impressionism tries to give upon canvas one absolute momentary view; the result is that when the beholder has himself actually been struck by that aspect, the picture has an extraordinary force and emotional value—like the vivid power of recalling the past possessed by smells. But, on the other hand, such a work is empty and trivial in the extreme; it is the photograph of a detached impression, not followed, as it would be in nature, by many variations of itself. An object so unusual is often unrecognizable, if the vision thus unnaturally isolated has never happened to come vividly into our own experience. The opposite school—what might be called *discursive* landscape painting—collects so many glimpses and gives so fully the sum of our positive observations of a par- ticular scene, that its work is sure to be perfectly intelligible and plain. If it seems unreal and uninteresting, that is because it is formless, like the collective object it represents, while it lacks that sensuous intensity and movement which might have made the reality stimulating.

The landscape contains, of course, innumerable things which have determinate forms; but if the attention is directed specif- ically to them, we have no longer what, by a curious limitation of the word, is called the love of nature. Not very long ago it was usual for painters of landscapes to introduce figures, build- ings, or ruins to add some human association to the beauty of the place. Or, if wildness and desolation were to be pictured, at least one weary wayfarer must be seen sitting upon a broken column. He might wear a toga and then be Marius among the ruins of Carthage. The landscape without figures would have seemed meaningless; the spectator would have sat in suspense awaiting something, as at the theatre when the curtain rises on an empty stage. The indeterminateness of the suggestions of an unhumanized scene was then felt as a defect; now we feel it rather as an exaltation. We need to be free; our emotion suffices us; we do not ask for a description of the object which interests us as a part of ourselves. We should blush to say so simple and obvious a thing as that to us "the mountains are a feeling"; nor should we think of apologizing for our romanticism as Byron did:

> I love not man the less but nature more
> From these our interviews, in which I steal,
> From all I may be, or have been before,
> To mingle with the universe, and feel
> What I can ne'er express.

This ability to rest in nature unadorned and to find entertainment in her aspects, is, of course, a great gain. Æsthetic education consists in training ourselves to see the maximum of beauty. To see it in the physical world, which must continually be about us, is a great progress toward that marriage of the imagination with the reality which is the goal of contemplation.

While we gain this mastery of the formless, however, we should not lose the more necessary capacity of seeing form in those things which happen to have it. In respect to most of those things which are determinate as well as natural, we are usually in that state of æsthetic unconsciousness which the peasant is in in respect to the landscape. We treat human life and its environment with the same utilitarian eye with which he regards the field and mountain. That is beautiful which is expressive of convenience and wealth; the rest is indifferent. If we mean by love of nature æsthetic delight in the world in which we casually live (and what can be more *natural* than man and all his arts?), we may say that the absolute love of *nature* hardly exists among us. What we love is the stimulation of our own personal emotions and dreams; and landscape appeals to us, as music does to those who have no sense for musical form.

There would seem to be no truth in the saying that the ancients loved nature less than we. They loved landscape less— less, at least, in proportion to their love of the definite things it contained. The vague and changing effects of the atmosphere, the masses of mountains, the infinite and living complexity of forests, did not fascinate them. They had not that preponderant taste for the indeterminate that makes the landscape a favourite subject of contemplation. But love of nature, and comprehension of her, they had in a most eminent degree; in fact, they actually made explicit that objectification of our own soul in her, which for the romantic poet remains a mere vague and shifting suggestion. What are the celestial gods, the nymphs, the fauns, the dryads, but the definite apperceptions of that haunting spirit which we think we see in the sky, the mountains, and the woods? We may think that our vague intuition grasps the truth of what their childish imagination turned into a fable. But our belief, if it is one, is just as fabulous, just as much a projection of human nature into material things; and if we renounce all positive conception of quasi-mental principles in nature, and reduce our moralizing of her to a poetic expression of our own sensations, then can we say that our verbal and illusive images are comparable as representations of the life of nature to the precision, variety, humour, and beauty of the Greek mythology?

§ 34. EXTENSIONS TO OBJECTS USUALLY NOT REGARDED ÆSTHET- ICALLY. It may not be superfluous to mention here certain anal- ogous fields where the human mind gives a series of unstable forms to objects in themselves indeterminate.[1] History, philos- ophy, natural as well as moral, and religion are evidently such fields. All theory is a subjective form given to an indeterminate material. The material is experience; and although each part of experience is, of course, perfectly definite in itself, and just that experience which it is, yet the recollection and relating together of the successive experiences is a function of the theoretical faculty. The systematic relations of things in time and space, and their dependence upon one another, are the work of our imagination. Theory can therefore never have the kind of truth which belongs to experience; as Hobbes has it, no discourse what- soever can end in absolute knowledge of fact.

It is conceivable that two different theories should be equally true in respect to the same facts. All that is required is that they should be equally complete schemes for the relation and predic- tion of the realities they deal with. The choice between them would be an arbitrary one, determined by personal bias, for the object being indeterminate, its elements can be apperceived as forming all kinds of unities. A theory is a form of apperception,

---

[1] When we speak of things definite in themselves, we of course mean things made definite by some human act of definition. The senses are in- struments that define and differentiate sensation; and the result of one operation is that definite object upon which the next operation is performed. The memory, for example, classifies in time what the senses may have classi- fied in space. We are nowhere concerned with objects other than objects of human experience, and the epithets, definite and indefinite, refer necessarily to their relation to our various categories of perception and comprehension.

and in applying it to the facts, although our first concern is naturally the adequacy of our instrument of comprehension, we are also influenced, more than we think, by the ease and pleasure with which we think in its terms, that is, by its beauty.

The case of two alternative theories of nature, both exhaustive and adequate, may seem somewhat imaginary. The human mind is, indeed, not rich and indeterminate enough to drive, as the saying is, many horses abreast; it wishes to have one general scheme of conception only, under which it strives to bring everything. Yet the philosophers, who are the scouts of common sense, have come in sight of this possibility of a variety of methods of dealing with the same facts. As at the basis of evolution generally there are many variations, only some of which remain fixed, so at the origin of conception there are many schemes; these are simultaneously developed, and at most stages of thought divide the intelligence among themselves. So much is thought of on one principle—say mechanically—and so much on another—say teleologically. In those minds only that have a speculative turn, that is, in whom the desire for unity of comprehension outruns practical exigencies, does the conflict become intolerable. In them one or another of these theories tends to swallow all experience, but is commonly incapable of doing so.

The final victory of a single philosophy is not yet won, because none as yet has proved adequate to all experience. If ever unity should be attained, our unanimity would not indicate that, as the popular fancy conceives it, the truth had been discovered; it would only indicate that the human mind had found a definitive way of classifying its experience. Very likely, if man still retained his inveterate habit of hypostatizing his ideas, that definitive scheme would be regarded as a representation of the objective relations of things; but no proof that it was so would ever be found, nor even any hint that there were external objects, not to speak of relations between them. As the objects are hypostatized percepts, so the relations are hypostatized processes of the human understanding.

To have reached a final philosophy would be only to have formulated the typical and satisfying form of human apperception; the view would remain a theory, an instrument of comprehension and survey fitted to the human eye; it would be for ever utterly heterogeneous from fact, utterly unrepresentative of any of those experiences which it would artificially connect and weave into a pattern. Mythology and theology are the most striking illustrations of this human method of incorporating much diffuse experience into graphic and picturesque ideas; but steady reflection will hardly allow us to see anything else in the theories of science and philosophy. These, too, are creatures of our intelligence, and have their only being in the movement of our thought, as they have their only justification in their fitness to our experience.

Long before we can attain, however, the ideal unification of experience under one theory, the various fields of thought demand provisional surveys; we are obliged to reflect on life in a variety of detached and unrelated acts, since neither can the whole material of life be ever given while we still live, nor can that which is given be impartially retained in the human memory. When omniscience was denied us, we were endowed with versatility. The picturesqueness of human thought may console us for its imperfection.

History, for instance, which passes for the account of facts, is in reality a collection of apperceptions of an indeterminate material; for even the material of history is not fact, but consists of memories and words subject to ever-varying interpretation. No historian can be without bias, because the bias defines the history. The memory in the first place is selective; official and other records are selective, and often intentionally partial. Monuments and ruins remain by chance. And when the historian has set himself to study these few relics of the past, the work of his own intelligence begins. He must have some guiding interest. A history is not an indiscriminate register of every known event; a file of newspapers is not an inspiration of Clio. A history is a view of the fortunes of some institution or person; it traces the development of some interest. This interest furnishes the standard by which the facts are selected, and their importance gauged. Then, after the facts are thus chosen, marshalled, and emphasized, comes the indication of causes and relations; and in this part of his work the historian plunges avowedly into speculation, and becomes a philosophical poet. Everything will then depend on his genius, on his principles, on his passions,— in a word, on his apperceptive forms. And the value of history is similar to that of poetry, and varies with the beauty, power, and adequacy of the form in which the indeterminate material of human life is presented.

§ 35. FURTHER DANGERS OF INDETERMINATENESS. The fondness of a race or epoch for any kind of effect is a natural expression of temperament and circumstances, and cannot be blamed or easily corrected. At the same time we may stop to consider some of the disadvantages of a taste for the indeterminate. We shall be registering a truth and at the same time, perhaps, giving some encouragement to that rebellion which we may inwardly feel against this too prevalent manner. The indeterminate is by its nature ambiguous; it is therefore obscure and uncertain in its effect, and if used, as in many arts it often is, to convey a meaning, must fail to do so unequivocally. Where a meaning is not to be conveyed, as in landscape, architecture, or music, the illusiveness of the form is not so objectionable: although in all these objects the tendency to observe forms and to demand them is a sign of increasing appreciation. The ignorant fail to see the forms of music, architecture, and landscape, and therefore are insensible to relative rank and technical values in these spheres; they regard the objects only as so many stimuli to emotion, as soothing or enlivening influences. But the sensuous and associative values of these things—especially of music—are so great, that even without an appreciation of form considerable beauty may be found in them.

In literature, however, where the sensuous value of the words is comparatively small, indeterminateness of form is fatal to beauty, and, if extreme, even to expressiveness. For meaning is conveyed by the *form* and order of words, not by the words themselves, and no precision of meaning can be reached without precision of style. Therefore no respectable writer is voluntarily obscure in the structure of his phrases—that is an abuse reserved for the clowns of literary fashion. But a book is a larger sentence, and if it is formless it fails to mean anything, for the same reason that an unformed collection of words means nothing. The chapters and verses may have said something, as loose words may have a known sense and a tone; but the book will have brought no message.

In fact, the absence of form in composition has two stages: that in which, as in the works of Emerson, significant fragments are collected, and no system, no total thought, constructed out of them; and secondly, that in which, as in the writings of the Symbolists of our time, all the significance is kept back in the individual words, or even in the syllables that compose them. This mosaic of word-values has, indeed, a possibility of effect, for the absence of form does not destroy materials, but, as we have observed, rather allows the attention to remain fixed upon them; and for this reason absence of sense is a means of accentuating beauty of sound and verbal suggestion. But this example shows how the tendency to neglect structure in literature is a tendency to surrender the use of language as an instrument of thought. The descent is easy from ambiguity to meaninglessness.

The indeterminate in form is also indeterminate in value. It needs completion by the mind of the observer and as this completion differs, the value of the result must vary. An indeterminate object is therefore beautiful to him who can make it so, and ugly to him who cannot. It appeals to a few, and to them diversely. In fact, the observer's own mind is the storehouse from which the beautiful form has to be drawn. If the form is not there, it cannot be applied to the half-finished object; it is like asking a man without skill to complete another man's composition. The indeterminate object therefore requires an active and well-equipped mind, and is otherwise without value.

It is furthermore unprofitable even to the mind which takes it up; it stimulates that mind to action, but it presents it with no new object. We can respond only with those forms of apperception which we already are accustomed to. A formless object cannot *inform* the mind, cannot mould it to a new habit. That happens only when the data, by their clear determination, compel the eye and imagination to follow new paths and see new relations. Then we are introduced to a new beauty, and enriched to that extent. But the indeterminate, like music to the sentimental, is a vague stimulus. It calls forth at random such ideas and memories as may lie to hand, stirring the mind, but leaving it undisciplined and unacquainted with any new object. This stirring, like that of the pool of Bethesda, may indeed have its virtue. A creative mind, already rich in experience and observation, may, under the influence of such a stimulus, dart into a new thought, and give birth to that with which it is already pregnant; but the fertilizing seed came from elsewhere, from study and admiration of those definite forms which nature contains, or which art, in imitation of nature, has conceived and brought to perfection.

§ 36. ILLUSION OF INFINITE PERFECTION. The great advantage, then, of indeterminate organization is that it cultivates that spontaneity, intelligence, and imagination without which many important objects would remain unintelligible, and because unintelligible, uninteresting. The beauty of landscape, the forms of religion and science, the types of human nature itself, are due to this apperceptive gift. Without it we should have a chaos;

but its patient and ever-fresh activity carves out of the fluid material a great variety of forms. An object which stimulates us to this activity, therefore, seems often to be more sublime and beautiful than one which presents to us a single unchanging form, however perfect. There seems to be a life and infinity in the incomplete, which the determinate excludes by its own completeness and petrifaction. And yet the effort in this very activity is to reach determination; we can only see beauty in so far as we introduce form. The instability of the form can be no advantage to a work of art; the determinate keeps constantly what the indeterminate reaches only in those moments in which the observer's imagination is especially propitious. If we feel a certain disappointment in the monotonous limits of a definite form and its eternal, unsympathizing message, might we not feel much more the melancholy transiency of those glimpses of beauty which elude us in the indeterminate? Might not the torment and uncertainty of this contemplation, with the self-consciousness it probably involves, more easily tire us than the quiet companionship of a constant object? May we not prefer the unchangeable to the irrecoverable?

We may; and the preference is one which we should all more clearly feel, were it not for an illusion, proper to the romantic temperament, which lends a mysterious charm to things which are indefinite and indefinable. It is the suggestion of infinite perfection. In reality, perfection is a synonym of finitude. Neither in nature nor in the fancy can anything be perfect except by realizing a definite type, which excludes all variation, and contrasts sharply with every other possibility of being. There is no perfection apart from a form of apperception or type; and there are as many kinds of perfection as there are types or forms of apperception latent in the mind.

Now these various perfections are mutually exclusive. Only in a kind of æsthetic orgy—in the madness of an intoxicated imagination—can we confuse them. As the Roman emperor wished that the Roman people had but a single neck, to murder them at one blow, so we may sometimes wish that all beauties had but one form, that we might behold them together. But in the nature of things beauties are incompatible. The spring cannot coexist with the autumn, nor day with night; what is beautiful in a child is hideous in a man, and *vice versa;* every age, every country, each sex, has a peculiar beauty, finite and incommunicable; the better it is attained the more completely it excludes every other. The same is evidently true of schools of art, of styles and languages, and of every effect whatsoever. It exists by its finitude and is great in proportion to its determination.

But there is a loose and somewhat helpless state of mind in which while we are incapable of realizing any particular thought or vision in its perfect clearness and absolute beauty, we nevertheless feel its haunting presence in the background of consciousness. And one reason why the idea cannot emerge from that obscurity is that it is not alone in the brain; a thousand other ideals, a thousand other plastic tendencies of thought, simmer there in confusion; and if any definite image is presented in response to that vague agitation of our soul, we feel its inadequacy to our need in spite of, or perhaps on account of, its own particular perfection. We then say that the classic does not satisfy us, and that the "Grecian cloys us with his perfectness." We are not capable of that concentrated and serious attention to one thing at a time which would enable us to sink into its being, and enjoy the intrinsic harmonies of its form, and the bliss of its immanent particular heaven; we flounder in the vague, but at the same time we are full of yearnings, of half-thoughts and semivisions, and the upward tendency and exaltation of our mood is emphatic and overpowering in proportion to our incapacity to think, speak, or imagine.

The sum of our incoherences has, however, an imposing volume and even, perhaps, a vague, general direction. We feel ourselves laden with an infinite burden; and what delights us most and seems to us to come nearest to the ideal is not what embodies any one possible form, but that which, by embodying none, suggests many, and stirs the mass of our inarticulate imagination with a pervasive thrill. Each thing, without being a beauty in itself, by stimulating our indeterminate emotion, seems to be a hint and expression of infinite beauty. That infinite perfection which cannot be realized, because it is self-contradictory, may be thus suggested, and on account of this suggestion an indeterminate effect may be regarded as higher, more significant, and more beautiful than any determinate one.

The illusion, however, is obvious. The infinite perfection suggested is an absurdity. What exists is a vague emotion, the objects of which, if they could emerge from the chaos of a confused imagination, would turn out to be a multitude of differently beautiful determinate things. This emotion of infinite perfection is the *materia prima—rudis indigestaque moles*—out of which attention, inspiration, and art can bring forth an infinity of particular perfections. Every æsthetic success, whether in contemplation or production, is the birth of one of these possibilities with which the sense of infinite perfection is pregnant. A work of art or an act of observation which remains indeterminate is, therefore, a failure, however much it may stir our emotion. It is a failure for two reasons. In the first place this emotion is seldom wholly pleasant; it is disquieting and perplexing; it brings a desire rather than a satisfaction. And in the second place, the emotion, not being embodied, fails to constitute the beauty of anything; and what we have is merely a sentiment, a consciousness that values are or might be there, but a failure to extricate those values, or to make them explicit and recognizable in an appropriate object.

These gropings after beauty have their worth as signs of æsthetic vitality and intimations of future possible accomplishment; but in themselves they are abortive, and mark the impotence of the imagination. Sentimentalism in the observer and romanticism in the artist are examples of this æsthetic incapacity. Whenever beauty is really seen and loved, it has a definite embodiment: the eye has precision, the work has style, and the object has perfection. The kind of perfection may indeed be new; and if the discovery of new perfections is to be called romanticism, then romanticism is the beginning of all æsthetic life. But if by romanticism we mean indulgence in confused suggestion and in the exhibition of turgid force, then there is evidently need of education, of attentive labour, to disentangle the beauties so vaguely felt, and give each its adequate embodiment. The breadth of our inspiration need not be lost in this process of clarification, for there is no limit to the number and variety of forms which the world may be made to wear; only, if it is to be appreciated as beautiful and not merely felt as unutterable, it must be seen as a kingdom of forms. Thus the works of Shakespeare give us a great variety, with a frequent marvellous precision of characterization, and the forms of his art are definite although its scope is great.

But by a curious anomaly, we are often expected to see the greatest expressiveness in what remains indeterminate, and in reality expresses nothing. As we have already observed, the sense of profundity and significance is a very detachable emotion; it can accompany a confused jumble of promptings quite as easily as it can a thorough comprehension of reality. The illusion of infinite perfection is peculiarly apt to produce this sensation. That illusion arises by the simultaneous awakening of many incipient thoughts and dim ideas; it stirs the depths of the mind as a wind stirs the thickets of a forest; and the unusual consciousness of the life and longing of the soul, brought by that gust of feeling, makes us recognize in the object a singular power, a mysterious meaning.

But the feeling of significance signifies little. All we have in this case is a potentiality of imagination; and only when this potentiality begins to be realized in definite ideas, does a real meaning, or any object which that meaning can mean, arise in the mind. The highest æsthetic good is not that vague potentiality, nor that contradictory, infinite perfection so strongly desired; it is the greatest number and variety of finite perfections. To learn to see in nature and to enshrine in the arts the typical forms of things; to study and recognize their variations; to domesticate the imagination in the world, so that everywhere beauty can be seen, and a hint found for artistic creation,—that is the goal of contemplation. Progress lies in the direction of discrimination and precision, not in that of formless emotion and reverie.

§ 37. ORGANIZED NATURE THE SOURCE OF APPERCEPTIVE FORMS; EXAMPLE OF SCULPTURE. The form of the material world is in one sense always perfectly definite, since the particles that compose it are at each moment in a given relative position; but a world that had no other form than that of such a constellation of atoms would remain chaotic to our perception, because we should not be able to survey it as a whole, or to keep our attention suspended evenly over its innumerable parts. According to evolutionary theory, mechanical necessity has, however, brought about a distribution and aggregation of elements such as, for our purposes, constitutes individual things. Certain systems of atoms move together as units; and these organisms reproduce themselves and recur so often in our environment, that our senses become accustomed to view their parts together. Their form becomes a natural and recognizable one. An order and sequence is established in our imagination by virtue of the order and sequence in which the corresponding impressions have come to our senses. We can remember, reproduce, and in reproducing vary, by kaleidoscopic tricks of the fancy, the forms in which our perceptions have come.

The mechanical organization of external nature is thus the source of apperceptive forms in the mind. Did not sensation, by a constant repetition of certain sequences, and a recurring exactitude of mathematical relations, keep our fancy clear and fresh, we should fall into an imaginative lethargy. Idealization would degenerate into indistinctness, and, by the dulling of our memory, we should dream a world daily more poor and vague.

This process is periodically observable in the history of the arts. The way in which the human figure, for instance, is depicted, is an indication of the way in which it is apperceived. The arts give back only so much of nature as the human eye has been able to master. The most primitive stage of drawing and sculpture presents man with his arms and legs, his ten fingers and ten toes, branching out into mid-air; the apperception of the body has been evidently practical and successive, and the artist sets down what he knows rather than any of the particular perceptions that conveyed that knowledge. Those perceptions are merged and lost in the haste to reach the practically useful concept of the object. By a naïve expression of the same principle, we find in some Assyrian drawings the eye seen from the front introduced into a face seen in profile, each element being represented in that form in which it was most easily observed and remembered. The development of Greek sculpture furnishes a good example of the gradual penetration of nature into the mind, of the slowly enriched apperception of the object. The quasi-Egyptian stiffness melts away, first from the bodies of the minor figures, afterwards of those of the gods, and finally the face is varied, and the hieratic smile almost disappears.[1]

But this progress has a near limit; once the most beautiful and inclusive apperception reached, once the best form caught at its best moment, the artist seems to have nothing more to do. To reproduce the imperfections of individuals seems wrong, when beauty, after all, is the thing desired. And the ideal, as caught by the master's inspiration, is more beautiful than anything his pupils can find for themselves in nature. From its summit, the art therefore declines in one of two directions. It either becomes academic, forsakes the study of nature, and degenerates into empty convention, or else it becomes ignoble, forsakes beauty, and sinks into a tasteless and unimaginative technique. The latter was the course of sculpture in ancient times, the former, with moments of reawakening, has been its dreadful fate among the moderns.

This reawakening has come whenever there has been a return to nature, for a new form of apperception and a new ideal. Of

[1] In the Ægina marbles the wounded and dying warriors still wear this Buddha-like expression: their bodies, although conventional, show a great progress in observation, compared with the impossible Athena in the centre with her sacred feet in Egyptian profile and her owl-like visage.

this return there is continual need in all the arts; without it our apperceptions grow thin and worn, and subject to the sway of tradition and fashion. We continue to judge about beauty, but we give up looking for it. The remedy is to go back to the reality, to study it patiently, to allow new aspects of it to work upon the mind, sink into it, and beget there an imaginative offspring after their own kind. Then a new art can appear, which, having the same origin in admiration for nature which the old art had, may hope to attain the same excellence in a new direction.

In fact, one of the dangers to which a modern artist is exposed is the seduction of his predecessors. The gropings of our muse, the distracted experiments of our architecture, often arise from the attraction of some historical school; we cannot work out our own style because we are hampered by the beauties of so many others. The result is an eclecticism, which, in spite of its great historical and psychological interest, is without æsthetic unity or permanent power to please. Thus the study of many schools of art may become an obstacle to proficiency in any.

§ 38. UTILITY THE PRINCIPLE OF ORGANIZATION IN NATURE. Utility (or, as it is now called, adaptation, and natural selection) organizes the material world into definite species and individuals. Only certain aggregations of matter are in equilibrium with the prevailing forces of the environment. Gravity, for instance, is in itself a chaotic force; it pulls all particles indiscriminately together without reference to the wholes into which the human eye may have grouped them. But the result is not chaos, because matter arranged in some ways is welded together by the very tendency which disintegrates it when arranged in other forms. These forms, selected by their congruity with gravity, are therefore fixed in nature, and become types. Thus the weight of the stones keeps the pyramid standing: here a certain shape has become a guarantee of permanence in the presence of a force in itself mechanical and undiscriminating. It is the utility of the pyramidal form—its fitness to stand—that has made it a type in building. The Egyptians merely repeated a process that they might have observed going on of itself in nature, who builds a pyramid in every hill, not indeed because she wishes to, or because pyramids are in any way an object of her action, but because she has no force which can easily dislodge matter that finds itself in that shape.

Such an accidental stability of structure is, in this moving

world, a sufficient principle of permanence and individuality.
The same mechanical principles, in more complex applications,
insure the persistence of animal forms and prevent any permanent deviation from them. What is called the principle of
self-preservation, and the final causes and substantial forms of
the Aristotelian philosophy, are descriptions of the result of this
operation. The tendency of everything to maintain and propa-
gate its nature is simply the inertia of a stable juxtaposition of
elements, which are not enough disturbed by ordinary accidents
to lose their equilibrium; while the incidence of a too great disturbance causes that disruption we call death, or that variation
of type, which, on account of its incapacity to establish itself
permanently, we call abnormal. Nature thus organizes herself
into recognizable species; and the æsthetic eye, studying her
forms, tends, as we have already shown, to bring the type within
even narrower limits than do the external exigencies of life.

§ 39. THE RELATION OF UTILITY TO BEAUTY. This natural harmony between utility and beauty, when its origin is not understood, is of course the subject of much perplexed and perplexing
theory. Sometimes we are told that utility is itself the essence
of beauty, that is, that our consciousness of the practical advantages of certain forms is the ground of our æsthetic admiration
of them. The horse's legs are said to be beautiful because they
are fit to run, the eye because it is made to see, the house because it is convenient to live in. An amusing application—which
might pass for a *reductio ad absurdum*—of this dense theory is
put by Xenophon into the mouth of Socrates. Comparing himself with a youth present at the same banquet, who was about to
receive the prize of beauty, Socrates declares himself more beautiful and more worthy of the crown. For utility makes beauty,
and eyes bulging out from the head like his are the most advantageous for seeing; nostrils wide and open to the air, like his,
most appropriate for smell; and a mouth large and voluminous,
like his, best fitted for both eating and kissing.[1]

Now since these things are, in fact, hideous, the theory that
shows they *ought to be* beautiful, is vain and ridiculous. But
that theory contains this truth: that had the utility of Socratic
features been so great that men of all other type must have
perished, Socrates would have been beautiful. He would have
represented the human type. The eye would have been then ac-

[1] *Symposium* of Xenophon, V.

customed to that form, the imagination would have taken it as the basis of its refinements, and accentuated its naturally effective points. The beautiful does not depend on the useful; it is constituted by the imagination in ignorance and contempt of practical advantage; but it is not independent of the necessary, for the necessary must also be the habitual and consequently the basis of the type, and of all its imaginative variations.

There are, moreover, at a late and derivative stage in our æsthetic judgment, certain cases in which the knowledge of fitness and utility enters into our sense of beauty. But it does so very indirectly, rather by convincing us that we should tolerate what practical conditions have imposed on an artist, by arousing admiration of his ingenuity, or by suggesting the interesting things themselves with which the object is known to be connected. Thus a cottage-chimney, stout and tall, with the smoke floating from it, pleases because we fancy it to mean a hearth, a rustic meal, and a comfortable family. But that is all extraneous association. The most ordinary way in which utility affects us is negatively; if we know a thing to be useless and fictitious, the uncomfortable haunting sense of waste and trickery prevents all enjoyment, and therefore banishes beauty. But this is also an adventitious complication. The intrinsic value of a form is in no way affected by it.

Opposed to this utilitarian theory stands the metaphysical one that would make the beauty or intrinsic rightness of things the source of their efficiency and of their power to survive. Taken literally, as it is generally meant, this idea must, from our point of view, appear preposterous. Beauty and rightness are relative to our judgment and emotion; they in no sense exist in nature or preside over her. She everywhere appears to move by mechanical law. The types of things exist by what, in relation to our approbation, is mere chance, and it is our faculties that must adapt themselves to our environment and not our environment to our faculties. Such is the naturalistic point of view which we have adopted.

To say, however, that beauty is in some sense the ground of practical fitness, need not seem to us wholly unmeaning. The fault of the Platonists who say things of this sort is seldom that of emptiness. They have an intuition; they have sometimes a strong sense of the facts of consciousness. But they turn their discoveries into so many revelations, and the veil of the infinite and absolute soon covers their little light of specific truth. Sometimes, after patient digging, the student comes upon the treasure of some simple fact, some common experience, beneath all their mystery and unction. And so it may be in this case. If we make allowances for the tendency to express experience in allegory and myth, we shall see that the idea of beauty and rationality presiding over nature and guiding her, as it were, for their own greater glory, is a projection and a writing large of a psychological principle.

The mind that perceives nature is the same that understands and enjoys her; indeed, these three functions are really elements of one process. There is therefore in the mere perceptibility of a thing a certain prophecy of its beauty; if it were not on the road to beauty, if it had no approach to fitness to our faculties of perception, the object would remain eternally unperceived. The sense, therefore, that the whole world is made to be food for the soul; that beauty is not only its own, but all things' excuse for being; that universal aspiration towards perfection is the key and secret of the world,—that sense is the poetical reverberation of a psychological fact—of the fact that our mind is an organism tending to unity, to unconsciousness of what is refractory to its action, and to assimilation and sympathetic transformation of what is kept within its sphere. The idea that nature could be governed by an aspiration towards beauty is, therefore, to be rejected as a confusion, but at the same time we must confess that this confusion is founded on a consciousness of the subjective relation between the perceptibility, rationality, and beauty of things.

§ 40. UTILITY THE PRINCIPLE OF ORGANIZATION IN THE ARTS. This subjective relation is, however, exceedingly loose. Most things that are perceivable are not perceived so distinctly as to be intelligible, nor so delightfully as to be beautiful. If our eye had infinite penetration, or our imagination infinite elasticity, this would not be the case; to see would then be to understand and to enjoy. As it is, the degree of determination needed for perception is much less than that needed for comprehension or ideality. Hence there is room for hypothesis and for art. As hypothesis organizes experiences imaginatively in ways in which observation has not been able to do, so art organizes objects in ways to which nature, perhaps, has never condescended.

The chief thing which the imitative arts add to nature is permanence, the lack of which is the saddest defect of many natural beauties. The forces which determine natural forms, therefore, determine also the forms of the imitative arts. But the non-imitative arts supply organisms different in kind from those which nature affords. If we seek the principle by which these objects are organized, we shall generally find that it is likewise utility. Architecture, for instance, has all its forms suggested by practical demands. Use requires our buildings to assume certain determinate forms; the mechanical properties of our materials, the exigency of shelter, light, accessibility, economy, and convenience, dictate the arrangements of our buildings.

Houses and temples have an evolution like that of animals and plants. Various forms arise by mechanical necessity, like the cave, or the shelter of overhanging boughs. These are perpetuated by a selection in which the needs and pleasures of man are the environment to which the structure must be adapted. Determinate forms thus establish themselves, and the eye becomes accustomed to them. The line of use, by habit of apperception, becomes the line of beauty. A striking example may be found in the pediment of the Greek temple and the gable of the northern house. The exigencies of climate determine these forms differently, but the eye in each case accepts what utility imposes. We admire height in one and breadth in the other, and we soon find the steep pediment heavy and the low gable awkward and mean.

It would be an error, however, to conclude that habit alone establishes the right proportion in these various types of building. We have the same intrinsic elements to consider as in natural forms. That is, besides the unity of type and correspondence of parts which custom establishes, there are certain appeals to more fundamental susceptibilities of the human eye and imagination. There is, for instance, the value of abstract form, determined by the pleasantness and harmony of implicated retinal or muscular tensions. Different structures contain or suggest more or less of this kind of beauty, and in that proportion may be called intrinsically better or worse. Thus artificial forms may be arranged in a hierarchy like natural ones, by reference to the absolute values of their contours and masses. Herein lies the superiority of a Greek to a Chinese vase, or of Gothic to Saracenic construction. Thus although every useful form is capable of proportion and beauty, when once its type is established, we cannot say that this beauty is always potentially equal; and an iron bridge, for instance, although it certainly possesses and daily acquires æsthetic interest, will probably never, on the average, equal a bridge of stone.

§ 41. FORM AND ADVENTITIOUS ORNAMENT. Beauty of form is the last to be found or admired in artificial as in natural objects. Time is needed to establish it, and training and nicety of perception to enjoy it. Motion or colour is what first interests a child in toys, as in animals; and the barbarian artist decorates long before he designs. The cave and wigwam are daubed with paint, or hung with trophies, before any pleasure is taken in their shape; and the appeal to the detached senses, and to associations of wealth and luxury, precedes by far the appeal to the perceptive harmonies of form. In music we observe the same gradation; first, we appreciate its sensuous and sentimental value; only with education can we enjoy its form. The plastic arts begin, therefore, with adventitious ornament and with symbolism. The æsthetic pleasure is in the richness of the material, the profusion of the ornament, the significance of the shape—in everything, rather than in the shape itself.

We have accordingly in works of art two independent sources of effect. The first is the useful form, which generates the type, and ultimately the beauty of form, when the type has been idealized by emphasizing its intrinsically pleasing traits. The second is the beauty of ornament, which comes from the excitement of the senses, or of the imagination, by colour, or by profusion or delicacy of detail. Historically, the latter is first developed, and applied to a form as yet merely useful. But the very presence of ornament attracts contemplation; the attention lavished on the object helps to fix its form in the mind, and to make us discriminate the less from the more graceful. The two kinds of beauty are then felt, and, yielding to that tendency to unity which the mind always betrays, we begin to subordinate and organize these two excellences. The ornament is distributed so as to emphasize the æsthetic essence of the form; to idealize it even more, by adding adventitious interests harmoniously to the intrinsic interest of the lines of structure.

There is here a great field, of course, for variety of combination and compromise. Some artists are fascinated by the decoration, and think of the structure merely as the background on which it can be most advantageously displayed. Others, of more austere taste, allow ornament only to emphasize the main lines of the design, or to conceal such inharmonious elements as nature or utility may prevent them from eliminating.[1] We may thus oscillate between decorative and structural motives, and only in one point, for each style, can we find the ideal equilibrium, in which the greatest strength and lucidity is combined with the greatest splendour.

A less subtle, but still very effective, combination is that hit upon by many oriental and Gothic architects, and found, also, by accident perhaps, in many buildings of the plateresque style; the ornament and structure are both presented with extreme emphasis, but locally divided; a vast rough wall, for instance, represents the one, and a profusion of mad ornament huddled around a central door or window represents the other.

Gothic architecture offers us in the pinnacle and flying buttress a striking example of the adoption of a mechanical feature, and its transformation into an element of beauty. Nothing could at first sight be more hopeless than the external half-arch propping the side of a pier, or the chimney-like weight of stones pressing it down from above; but a courageous acceptance of these necessities, and a submissive study of their form, revealed a new and strange effect: the bewildering and stimulating intricacy of masses suspended in mid-air; the profusion of line, variety of surface, and picturesqueness of light and shade. It needed but a little applied ornament judiciously distributed; a moulding in the arches; a florid canopy and statue amid the buttresses; a few grinning monsters leaning out of unexpected nooks; a leafy

---

[1] It is a superstition to suppose that a refined taste would necessarily find the actual and useful to be the perfect; to conceal structure is as legitimate as to emphasize it, and for the same reason. We emphasize in the direction of abstract beauty, in the direction of absolute pleasure; and we conceal or eliminate in the same direction. The most exquisite Greek taste, for instance, preferred to drape the lower part of the female figure, as in the Venus of Milo; also in men to shave the hair of the face and body, in order to maintain the purity and strength of the lines. In the one case we conceal structure, in the other we reveal it, modifying nature into greater sympathy with our faculties of perception. For, after all, it must be remembered that beauty, or pleasure to be given to the eye, is not a guiding principle in the world of nature or in that of the practical arts. The beauty is in nature a result of the functional adaptation of our senses and imagination to the mechanical products of our environment. This adaptation is never complete, and there is, accordingly, room for the fine arts, in which beauty is a result of the intentional adaptation of mechanical forms to the functions which our senses and imagination already have acquired. This watchful subservience to our æsthetic demands is the essence of fine art. Nature is the basis, but man is the goal.

budding of the topmost pinnacles; a piercing here and there of
some little gallery, parapet, or turret into lacework against
the sky—and the building became a poem, an inexhaustible
emotion. Add some passing cloud casting its moving shadow over
the pile, add the circling of birds about the towers, and you have
an unforgettable type of beauty; not perhaps the noblest, sanest,
or most enduring, but one for the existence of which the imagination is richer, and the world more interesting.

In this manner we accept the forms imposed upon us by
utility, and train ourselves to apperceive their potential beauty.
Familiarity breeds contempt only when it breeds inattention.
When the mind is absorbed and dominated by its perceptions,
it incorporates into them more and more of its own functional
values, and makes them ultimately beautiful and expressive.
Thus no language can be ugly to those who speak it well, no
religion unmeaning to those who have learned to pour their
life into its moulds.

Of course these forms vary in intrinsic excellence; they are by
their specific character more or less fit and facile for the average
mind. But the man and the age are rare who can choose their
own path; we have generally only a choice between going ahead
in the direction already chosen, or halting and blocking the path
for others. The only kind of reform usually possible is reform
from within; a more intimate study and more intelligent use of
the traditional forms. Disaster follows rebellion against tradition
or against utility, which are the basis and root of our taste and
progress. But, within the given school, and as exponents of its
spirit, we can adapt and perfect our works, if haply we are better
inspired than our predecessors. For the better we know a given
thing, and the more we perceive its strong and weak points, the
more capable we are of idealizing it.

§ 42. FORM IN WORDS. The main effect of language consists in
its meaning, in the ideas which it expresses. But no expression is
possible without a presentation, and this presentation must have
a form. This form of the instrument of expression is itself an
element of effect, although in practical life we may overlook it
in our haste to attend to the meaning it conveys. It is, moreover,
a condition of the kind of expression possible, and often determines the manner in which the object suggested shall be apperceived. No word has the exact value of any other in the same

or in another language.[1] But the intrinsic effect of language does not stop there. The single word is but a stage in the series of formations which constitute language, and which preserve for men the fruit of their experience, distilled and concentrated into a symbol.

This formation begins with the elementary sounds themselves, which have to be discriminated and combined to make recognizable symbols. The evolution of these symbols goes on spontaneously, suggested by our tendency to utter all manner of sounds, and preserved by the ease with which the ear discriminates these sounds when made. Speech would be an absolute and unrelated art, like music, were it not controlled by utility. The sounds have indeed no resemblance to the objects they symbolize; but before the system of sounds can represent the system of objects, there has to be a correspondence in the groupings of both. The structure of language, unlike that of music, thus becomes a mirror of the structure of the world as presented to the intelligence.

Grammar, philosophically studied, is akin to the deepest metaphysics, because in revealing the constitution of speech, it reveals the constitution of thought, and the hierarchy of those categories by which we conceive the world. It is by virtue of this parallel development that language has its function of expressing experience with exactness, and the poet—to whom language is an instrument of art—has to employ it also with a constant reference to meaning and veracity; that is, he must be a master of experience before he can become a true master of words. Nevertheless, language is primarily a sort of music, and the beautiful effects which it produces are due to its own structure, giving, as it crystallizes in a new fashion, an unforeseen form to experience.

Poets may be divided into two classes: the musicians and the psychologists. The first are masters of significant language as harmony; they know what notes to sound together and in

[1] Not only are words untranslatable when the exact object has no name in another language, as "home" or "mon ami," but even when the object is the same, the attitude toward it, incorporated in one word, cannot be rendered by another. Thus, to my sense, "bread" is as inadequate a translation of the human intensity of the Spanish "pan" as "Dios" is of the awful mystery of the English "God." This latter word does not designate an object at all, but a sentiment, a psychosis, not to say a whole chapter of religious history. English is remarkable for the intensity and variety of the colour of its words. No language, I believe, has so many words specifically poetic.

succession; they can produce, by the marshalling of sounds and images, by the fugue of passion and the snap of wit, a thousand brilliant effects out of old materials. The Ciceronian orator, the epigrammatic, lyric, and elegiac poets, give examples of this art. The psychologists, on the other hand, gain their effect not by the intrinsic mastery of language, but by the closer adaptation of it to things. The dramatic poets naturally furnish an illustration.

But however transparent we may wish to make our language, however little we may call for its intrinsic effects, and direct our attention exclusively to its expressiveness, we cannot avoid the limitations of our particular medium. The character of the tongue a man speaks, and the degree of his skill in speaking it, must always count enormously in the æsthetic value of his compositions; no skill in observation, no depth of thought or feeling, but is spoiled by a bad style and enhanced by a good one. The diversities of tongues and their irreducible æsthetic values, begins with the very sound of the letters, with the mode of utterance, and the characteristic inflections of the voice; notice, for instance, the effect of the French of these lines of Alfred de Musset,

> Jamais deux yeux plus doux n'ont du ciel le plus pur
> Sondé la profondeur et réfléchi l'azur.

and compare with its flute-like and treble quality the breadth, depth, and volume of the German in this inimitable stanza of Goethe's:

> Ueber allen Gipfeln
> Ist Ruh,
> In allen Wipfeln
> Spürest du
> Kaum einen Hauch;
> Die Vögelein schweigen im Walde.
> Warte nur, balde
> Ruhest du auch.

Even if the same tune could be played on both these vocal instruments, the difference in their *timbre* would make the value of the melody entirely distinct in each case.

§ 43. SYNTACTICAL FORM. The known impossibility of adequate translation appears here at the basis of language. The other diversities are superadded upon this diversity of sound. The syntax is the next source of effect. What could be better than Homer, or what worse than almost any translation of him? And this holds even of languages so closely allied as the Indo-European, which, after all, have certain correspondences of syntax and inflection. If there could be a language with other parts of speech than ours,—a language without nouns, for instance,—how would that grasp of experience, that picture of the world, which all our literature contains, be reproduced in it? Whatever beauties that language might be susceptible of, none of the effects produced on us, I will not say by poets, but even by nature itself, could be expressed in it.

Nor is such a language inconceivable. Instead of summarizing all our experiences of a thing by one word, its name, we should have to recall by appropriate adjectives the various sensations we had received from it; the objects we think of would be disintegrated, or, rather, would never have been unified. For "sun," they would say "high, yellow, dazzling, round, slowly moving," and the enumeration of these qualities (as we call them), without any suggestion of a unity at their source, might give a more vivid and profound, if more cumbrous, representation of the facts. But how could the machinery of such an imagination be capable of repeating the effects of ours, when the objects to us most obvious and real would be to those minds utterly indescribable?

The same diversity appears in the languages we ordinarily know, only in a lesser degree. The presence or absence of case-endings in nouns and adjectives, their difference of gender, the richness of inflections in the verbs, the frequency of particles and conjunctions,—all these characteristics make one language differ from another entirely in genius and capacity of expression. Greek is probably the best of all languages in melody, richness, elasticity, and simplicity; so much so, that in spite of its complex inflections, when once a vocabulary is acquired, it is more easy and natural for a modern than his ancestral Latin itself. Latin is the stiffer tongue; it is by nature at once laconic and grandiloquent, and the exceptional condensation and transposition of which it is capable make its effects entirely foreign to a modern, scarcely inflected, tongue. Take, for instance, these lines of Horace:

> me tabula sacer
> votiva paries indicat uvida
> suspendisse potenti
> vestimenta maris deo,

or these of Lucretius:

> Jamque caput quassans grandis suspirat arator
> Crebrius incassum magnum cecidisse laborem.

What conglomerate plebeian speech of our time could utter the stately grandeur of these Lucretian words, every one of which is noble, and wears the toga?

As a substitute for the inimitable interpenetration of the words in the Horatian strophe, we might have the external links of rhyme; and it seems, in fact, to be a justification of rhyme, that besides contributing something to melody and to the distribution of parts, it gives an artificial relationship to the phrases between which it obtains, which, but for it, would run away from one another in a rapid and irrevocable flux. In such a form as the sonnet, for instance, we have, by dint of assonance, a real unity forced upon the thought; for a sonnet in which the thought is not distributed appropriately to the structure of the verse, has no excuse for being a sonnet. By virtue of this inter-relation of parts, the sonnet, the *non plus ultra* of rhyme, is the most classic of modern poetical forms: much more classic in spirit than blank verse, which lacks almost entirely the power of synthesizing the phrase, and making the unexpected seem the inevitable.

This beauty given to the ancients by the syntax of their language, the moderns can only attain by the combination of their rhymes. It is a bad substitute perhaps, but better than the total absence of form, favoured by the atomic character of our words, and the flat juxtaposition of our clauses. The art which was capable of making a gem of every prose sentence,—the art which, carried, perhaps, to a pitch at which it became too conscious, made the phrases of Tacitus a series of cameos,—that art is inapplicable to our looser medium; we cannot give clay the finish and nicety of marble. Our poetry and speech in general, therefore, start out upon a lower level; the same effort will not, with this instrument, attain the same beauty. If equal beauty is ever attained, it comes from the wealth of suggestion, or the refinement of sentiment. The art of words remains hopelessly inferior. And what best proves this, is that when, as in our time, a reawakening of the love of beauty has prompted a refinement of our poetical language, we pass so soon into extravagance, obscurity, and affectation. Our modern languages are not susceptible of great formal beauty.

§ 44. LITERARY FORM. THE PLOT. The forms of composition in verse and prose which are practised in each language are further organizations of words, and have formal values. The most exacting of these forms and that which has been carried to the greatest perfection is the drama; but it belongs to rhetoric and poetics to investigate the nature of these effects, and we have here sufficiently indicated the principle which underlies them. The plot, which Aristotle makes, and very justly, the most important element in the effect of a drama, is the formal element of the drama as such: the ethos and sentiments are the expression, and the versification, music, and stage settings are the materials. It is in harmony with the romantic tendency of modern times that modern dramatists—Shakespeare as well as Molière, Calderon, and the rest—excel in ethos rather than in plot; for it is the evident characteristic of modern genius to study and enjoy expression,—the suggestion of the not-given,—rather than form, the harmony of the given.

Ethos is interesting mainly for the personal observations which it summarizes and reveals, or for the appeal to one's own actual or imaginative experience; it is portrait-painting, and enshrines something we love independently of the charm which at this moment and in this place it exercises over us. It appeals to our affections; it does not form them. But the plot is the synthesis of actions, and is a reproduction of those experiences from which our notion of men and things is originally derived; for character can never be observed in the world except as manifested in action.

Indeed, it would be more fundamentally accurate to say that a character is a symbol and mental abbreviation for a peculiar set of acts, than to say that acts are a manifestation of character. For the acts are the data, and the character the inferred principle, and a principle, in spite of its name, is never more than a description *a posteriori,* and a summary of what is subsumed under it. The plot, moreover, is what gives individuality to the play, and exercises invention; it is, as Aristotle again says, the most difficult portion of dramatic art, and that for which practice and training are most indispensable. And this plot, giving by its nature a certain picture of human experience, involves and suggests the ethos of its actors.

What the great characterizers, like Shakespeare, do, is simply to elaborate and develope (perhaps far beyond the necessities of the plot) the suggestion of human individuality which that plot contains. It is as if, having drawn from daily observation some knowledge of the tempers of our friends, we represented them saying and doing all manner of ultra-characteristic things, and in an occasional soliloquy laying bare, even more clearly than by any possible action, that character which their observed behaviour had led us to impute to them. This is an ingenious and fascinating invention, and delights us with the clear discovery of a hidden personality; but the serious and equable development of a plot has a more stable worth in its greater similarity to life, which allows us to see other men's minds through the medium of events, and not events through the medium of other men's minds.

§ 45. CHARACTER AS AN ÆSTHETIC FORM. We have just come upon one of the unities most coveted in our literature, and most valued by us when attained,—the portrait, the individuality, the character. The construction of a plot we call invention, but that of a character we dignify with the name of creation. It may therefore not be amiss, in finishing our discussion of form, to devote a few pages to the psychology of character-drawing. How does the unity we call a character arise, how is it described, and what is the basis of its effect?

We may set it down at once as evident that we have here a case of the type: the similarities of various persons are amalgamated, their differences cancelled, and in the resulting percept those traits emphasized which have particularly pleased or interested us. This, in the abstract, may serve for a description of the origin of an idea of character quite as well as of an idea of physical form. But the different nature of the material—the fact that a character is not a presentation to sense, but a rationalistic synthesis of successive acts and feelings, not combinable into any image—makes such a description much more unsatisfying in this case than in that of material forms. We cannot understand exactly how these summations and cancellings take place when we are not dealing with a visible object. And we may even feel that there is a wholeness and inwardness about the development of certain ideal characters, that makes such a treatment of them fundamentally false and artificial. The subjective element, the spontaneous expression of our own passion and will, here counts for so much, that the creation of an ideal character becomes a new and peculiar problem.

There is, however, a way of conceiving and delineating character which still bears a close resemblance to the process by which the imagination produces the type of any physical species. We may gather, for instance, about the nucleus of a word, designating some human condition or occupation, a number of detached observations. We may keep a note-book in our memory, or even in our pocket, with studious observations of the language, manners, dress, gesture, and history of the people we meet, classifying our statistics under such heads as innkeepers, soldiers, house-maids, governesses, adventuresses, Germans, Frenchmen, Italians, Americans, actors, priests, and professors. And then, when occasion offers, to describe, or to put into a book or a play, any one of these types, all we have to do is to look over our notes, to select according to the needs of the moment, and if we are skilful in reproduction, to obtain by that means a life-like image of the sort of person we wish to represent.

This process, which novelists and playwrights may go through deliberately, we all carry on involuntarily. At every moment experience is leaving in our minds some trait, some expression, some image, which will remain there attached to the name of a person, a class, or a nationality. Our likes and dislikes, our summary judgments on whole categories of men, are nothing but the distinct survival of some such impression. These traits have vivacity. If the picture they draw is one-sided and inadequate, the sensation they recall may be vivid, and suggestive of many other aspects of the thing. Thus the epithets in Homer, although they are often far from describing the essence of the object—γλαυκῶπις ᾿Αθήνη, εὐκνήμιδες ᾿Αχαιοί—seem to recall a sensation, and to give vitality to the narrative. By bringing you, through one sense, into the presence of the object, they give you that same hint of further discovery, that same expectation of experience, which we have at the sight of whatever we call real.

The graphic power of this method of observation and aggregation of characteristic traits is thus seen to be great. But it is not by this method that the most famous or most living characters have been conceived. This method gives the average, or at most the salient, points of the type, but the great characters of poetry—a Hamlet, a Don Quixote, an Achilles—are no averages, they are not even a collection of salient traits common to certain classes of men. They seem to be persons; that is, their actions and words seem to spring from the inward nature of an individual soul. Goethe is reported to have said that he conceived the character of his Gretchen entirely without observation of originals. And, indeed, he would probably not have found any. His creation rather is the original to which we may occasionally think we see some likeness in real maidens. It is the fiction here that is the standard of naturalness. And on this, as on so many occasions, we may repeat the saying that poetry is truer than history. Perhaps no actual maid ever spoke and acted so naturally as this imaginary one.

If we think there is any paradox in these assertions, we should reflect that the standard of naturalness, individuality, and truth is in us. A real person seems to us to have character and consistency when his behaviour is such as to impress a definite and simple image upon our mind. In themselves, if we could count all their undiscovered springs of action, all men have character and consistency alike: all are equally fit to be types. But their characters are not equally intelligible to us, their behaviour is not equally deducible, and their motives not equally appreciable. Those who appeal most to us, either in themselves or by the emphasis they borrow from their similarity to other individuals, are those we remember and regard as the centres around which variations oscillate. These men are natural: all others are more or less eccentric.

§ 46. IDEAL CHARACTERS. The standard of naturalness being thus subjective, and determined by the laws of our imagination, we can understand why a spontaneous creation of the mind can be more striking and living than any reality, or any abstraction from realities. The artist can invent a form which, by its adaptation to the imagination, lodges there, and becomes a point of reference for all observations, and a standard of naturalness and beauty. A type may be introduced to the mind suddenly, by the chance presentation of a form that by its intrinsic impressiveness and imaginative coherence, acquires that pre-eminence which custom, or the mutual reinforcement of converging experiences, ordinarily gives to empirical percepts.

This method of originating types is what we ordinarily describe as artistic creation. The name indicates the suddenness, originality, and individuality of the conception thus attained. What we call idealization is often a case of it. In idealization proper, however, what happens is the elimination of individual eccentricities; the result is abstract, and consequently meagre. This meagreness is often felt to be a greater disadvantage than the accidental and picturesque imperfection of real individuals, and the artist therefore turns to the brute fact, and studies and reproduces that with indiscriminate attention, rather than lose strength and individuality in the presentation of an insipid type. He seems forced to a choice between an abstract beauty and an unlovely example.

But the great and masterful presentations of the ideal are somehow neither the one nor the other. They present ideal beauty with just that definiteness with which nature herself sometimes presents it. When we come in a crowd upon an incomparably beautiful face, we know it immediately as an embodiment of the ideal; while it contains the type,—for if it did not we should find it monstrous and grotesque,—it clothes that type in a peculiar splendour of form, colour, and expression. It has an individuality. And just so the imaginary figures of poetry and plastic art may have an individuality given them by the happy affinities of their elements in the imagination. They are not idealizations, they are spontaneous variations, which can arise in the mind quite as easily as in the world. They spring up in

> The wreathèd trellis of a working brain;
> . . . With all the gardner fancy e'er could feign
> Who, breeding flowers, will never breed the same.

Imagination, in a word, generates as well as abstracts; it observes, combines, and cancels; but it also dreams. Spontaneous syntheses arise in it which are not mathematical averages of the images it receives from sense; they are effects of diffused excitements left in the brain by sensations. These excitements vary constantly in their various renewals, and occasionally take such a form that the soul is surprised by the inward vision of an unexampled beauty. If this inward vision is clear and steady, we have an æsthetic inspiration, a vocation to create; and if we can also command the technique of an appropriate art, we shall hasten to embody that inspiration, and realize an ideal. This ideal will be gradually recognized as supremely beautiful for the same reason that the object, had it been presented in the real world, would have been recognized as supremely beautiful; because while embodying a known type of form,—being, that is, a proper man, animal, or vegetable,—it possessed in an extraordinary degree those direct charms which most subjugate our attention.

Imaginary forms then differ in dignity and beauty not according to their closeness to fact or type in nature, but according to the ease with which the normal imagination reproduces the synthesis they contain. To add wings to a man has always been a natural fancy; because man can easily imagine himself to fly, and the idea is delightful to him. The winged man is therefore a form generally recognized as beautiful; although it can happen, as it did to Michael Angelo, that our appreciation of the actual form of the human body should be too keen and overmastering to allow us to relish even so charming and imaginative an extravagance. The centaur is another beautiful monster. The imagination can easily follow the synthesis of the dream in which horse and man melted into one, and first gave the glorious suggestion of their united vitality.

The same condition determines the worth of imaginary personalities. From the gods to the characters of comedy, all are, in proportion to their beauty, natural and exhilarating expressions of possible human activity. We sometimes remould visible forms into imaginary creatures; but our originality in this respect is meagre compared with the profusion of images of action which arise in us, both asleep and awake; we constantly dream of new situations, extravagant adventures, and exaggerated passions. Even our soberer thoughts are very much given to following the possible fortunes of some enterprise, and foretasting the satisfactions of love and ambition. The mind is therefore particularly sensitive to pictures of action and character; we are easily induced to follow the fortunes of any hero, and share his sentiments.

Our will, as Descartes said in a different context, is infinite, while our intelligence is finite; we follow experience pretty closely in our ideas of things, and even the furniture of fairyland bears a sad resemblance to that of earth; but there is no limit to the elasticity of our passion; and we love to fancy ourselves kings and beggars, saints and villains, young and old, happy and unhappy. There seems to be a boundless capacity of development in each of us, which the circumstances of life determine to a narrow channel; and we like to revenge ourselves in our reveries for this imputed limitation, by classifying ourselves with all that we are not, but might so easily have been. We are full of sympathy for every manifestation of life, however unusual; and even the conception of infinite knowledge and happiness—than which nothing could be more removed from our condition or more unrealizable to our fancy—remains eternally interesting to us.

The poet, therefore, who wishes to delineate a character need not keep a note-book. There is a quicker road to the heart—if he has the gift to find it. Probably his readers will not themselves have kept note-books, and his elaborate observations will only be effective when he describes something which they also happen to have noticed. The typical characters describable by the empirical method are therefore few: the miser, the lover, the old nurse, the ingénue, and the other types of traditional comedy. Any greater specification would appeal only to a small audience for a short time, because the characteristics depicted would no longer exist to be recognized. But whatever experience a poet's hearers may have had, they are men. They will have certain imaginative capacities to conceive and admire those forms of character and action which, although never actually found, are felt by each man to express what he himself might and would have been, had circumstances been more favourable.

The poet has only to study himself, and the art of expressing his own ideals, to find that he has expressed those of other people. He has but to enact in himself the part of each of his personages, and if he possesses that pliability and that definiteness of imagination which together make genius, he may express for his fellows those inward tendencies which in them have remained painfully dumb. He will be hailed as master of the human soul. He may know nothing of men, he may have almost no experience; but his creations will pass for models of naturalness, and for types of humanity. Their names will be in every one's mouth, and the lives of many generations will be enriched by the vision, one might almost say by the friendship, of these imaginary beings. They have individuality without having reality, because individuality is a thing acquired in the mind by the congeries of its impressions. They have power, also, because that depends on the appropriateness of a stimulus to touch the springs of reaction in the soul. And they of course have beauty, because in them is embodied the greatest of our imaginative delights,— that of giving body to our latent capacities, and of wandering, without the strain and contradiction of actual existence, into all forms of possible being.

§ 47. THE RELIGIOUS IMAGINATION. The greatest of these creations have not been the work of any one man. They have been the slow product of the pious and poetic imagination. Starting from some personification of nature or some memory of a great man, the popular and priestly tradition has refined and developed the ideal; it has made it an expression of men's aspiration and a counterpart of their need. The devotion of each tribe, shrine, and psalmist has added some attribute to the god or some parable to his legend; and thus, around the kernel of some original divine function, the imagination of a people has gathered every possible expression of it, creating a complete and beautiful personality, with its history, its character, and its gifts. No poet has ever equalled the perfection or significance of these religious creations. The greatest characters of fiction are uninteresting and unreal compared with the conceptions of the gods; so much so that men have believed that their gods have objective reality.

The forms men see in dreams might have been a reason for believing in vague and disquieting ghosts; but the belief in individual and well-defined divinities, with which the visions of the dreams might be identified, is obviously due to the intrinsic coherence and impressiveness of the conception of those deities. The vision would never have suggested the legend and attributes of the god; but when the figure of the god was once imaginatively conceived, and his name and aspect fixed in the imagination, it would be easy to recognize him in any hallucination, or to interpret any event as due to his power. These manifestations, which constitute the evidence of his actual existence, can be regarded as manifestations of him, rather than of a vague, unknown power, only when the imagination already possesses a vivid picture of him, and of his appropriate functions. This picture is the work of a spontaneous fancy.

No doubt, when the belief is once specified, and the special and intelligible god is distinguished in the night and horror of the all-pervading natural power, the belief in his reality helps to concentrate our attention on his nature, and thus to develope and enrich our idea. The belief in the reality of an ideal personality brings about its further idealization. Had it ever occurred to any Greek seer to attribute events to the influence of Achilles, or to offer sacrifices to him in the heat of the enthusiasm kindled by the thought of his beauty and virtue, the legend of Achilles, now become a god, would have grown and deepened; it would have been moralized like the legend of Hercules, or naturalized like that of Persephone, and what is now but a poetic character of extraordinary force and sublimity would have become the adored patron of generation after generation, and a manifestation of the divine man.

Achilles would then have been as significant and unforgettable a figure as Apollo or his sister, as Zeus, Athena, and the other greater gods. If ever, while that phase of religion lasted, his character had been obscured and his features dimmed, he would have been recreated by every new votary: poets would never have tired of singing his praises, or sculptors of rendering his form. When, after the hero had been the centre and subject of so much imaginative labour, the belief in his reality lapsed, to be transferred to some other conception of cosmic power, he would have remained an ideal of poetry and art, and a formative influence

of all cultivated minds. This he is still, like all the great creations of avowed fiction, but he would have been immensely more
so, had belief in his reality kept the creative imagination con-
tinuously intent upon his nature.

The reader can hardly fail to see that all this applies with
equal force to the Christian conception of the sacred personalities. Christ, the Virgin Mary, and the saints may have been
exactly what our imagination pictures them to be; that is
entirely possible; nor can I see that it is impossible that the conceptions of other religions might themselves have actual counter-
parts somewhere in the universe. That is a question of faith and
empirical evidence with which we are not here concerned. But
however descriptive of truth our conceptions may be, they have
evidently grown up in our minds by an inward process of development. The materials of history and tradition have been
melted and recast by the devout imagination into those figures
in the presence of which our piety lives.

That is the reason why the reconstructed logical gods of the
metaphysicians are always an offence and a mockery to the religious consciousness. There is here, too, a bare possibility that
some one of these absolutes may be a representation of the
truth; but the method by which this representation is acquired
is violent and artificial; while the traditional conception of God
is the spontaneous embodiment of passionate contemplation and
long experience.

As the God of religion differs from that of metaphysics, so
does the Christ of tradition differ from that of our critical histo-
rians. Even if we took the literal narrative of the Gospels and
accepted it as all we could know of Christ, without allowing
ourselves any imaginative interpretation of the central figure, we
should get an ideal of him, I will not say very different from that
of St. Francis or St. Theresa, but even from that of the English
prayer-book. The Christ men have loved and adored is an ideal
of their own hearts, the construction of an ever-present personality, living and intimately understood, out of the fragments
of story and doctrine connected with a name. This subjective
image has inspired all the prayers, all the conversions, all the
penances, charities, and sacrifices, as well as half the art of the
Christian world.

The Virgin Mary, whose legend is so meagre, but whose power
over the Catholic imagination is so great, is an even clearer illustration of this inward building up of an ideal form. Everything
is here spontaneous sympathetic expansion of two given events:

the incarnation and the crucifixion. The figure of the Virgin, found in these mighty scenes, is gradually clarified and developed, until we come to the thought on the one hand of her freedom from original sin, and on the other to that of her universal maternity. We thus attain the conception of one of the noblest of conceivable rôles and of one of the most beautiful of characters. It is a pity that a foolish iconoclasm should so long have deprived the Protestant mind of the contemplation of this ideal.

Perhaps it is a sign of the average imaginative dulness or fatigue of certain races and epochs that they so readily abandon these supreme creations. For, if we are hopeful, why should we not believe that the best we can fancy is also the truest; and if we are distrustful in general of our prophetic gifts, why should we cling only to the most mean and formless of our illusions? From the beginning to the end of our perceptive and imaginative activity, we are synthesizing the material of experience into unities the independent reality of which is beyond proof, nay, beyond the possibility of a shadow of evidence. And yet the life of intelligence, like the joy of contemplation, lies entirely in the formation and inter-relation of these unities. This activity yields us all the objects with which we can deal, and endows them with the finer and more intimate part of their beauty. The most perfect of these forms, judged by its affinity to our powers and its stability in the presence of our experience, is the one with which we should be content; no other kind of veracity could add to its value.

The greatest feats of synthesis which the human mind has yet accomplished will, indeed, be probably surpassed and all ideals yet formed be superseded, because they were not based upon enough experience, or did not fit that experience with adequate precision. It is also possible that changes in the character of the facts, or in the powers of intelligence, should necessitate a continual reconstruction of our world. But unless human nature suffers an inconceivable change, the chief intellectual and æsthetic value of our ideas will always come from the creative action of the imagination.

PART IV

EXPRESSION

§ 48. EXPRESSION DEFINED. We have found in the beauty of material and form the objectification of certain pleasures connected with the process of direct perception, with the formation, in the one case of a sensation, or quality, in the other of a synthesis of sensations or qualities. But the human consciousness is not a perfectly clear mirror, with distinct boundaries and clear-cut images, determinate in number and exhaustively perceived. Our ideas half emerge for a moment from the dim continuum of vital feeling and diffused sense, and are hardly fixed before they are changed and transformed, by the shifting of attention and the perception of new relations, into ideas of really different objects. This fluidity of the mind would make reflection impossible, did we not fix in words and other symbols certain abstract contents; we thus become capable of recognizing in one perception the repetition of another, and of recognizing in certain recurrences of impressions a persistent object. This discrimination and classification of the contents of consciousness is the work of perception and understanding, and the pleasures that accompany these activities make the beauty of the sensible world.

But our hold upon our thoughts extends even further. We not only construct visible unities and recognizable types, but remain aware of their affinities to what is not at the time perceived; that is, we find in them a certain tendency and quality, not original to them, a meaning and a tone, which upon investigation we shall see to have been the proper characteristics of other objects and feelings, associated with them once in our experience. The hushed reverberations of these associated feelings continue in the brain, and by modifying our present reaction, colour the image upon which our attention is fixed. The quality thus acquired by objects through association is what we call their expression. Whereas in form or material there is one object with its emotional effect, in expression there are two, and the emotional effect belongs to the character of the second or suggested one. Expression may thus make beautiful by suggestion things in themselves indifferent, or it may come to heighten the beauty which they already possess.

Expression is not always distinguishable in consciousness from the value of material or form, because we do not always have a distinguishable memory of the related idea which the expressiveness implies. When we have such a memory, as at the sight of some once frequented garden, we clearly and spontaneously attribute our emotion to the memory and not to the present fact which it beautifies. The revival of a pleasure and its embodiment in a present object which in itself might have been indifferent, is here patent and acknowledged.

The distinctness of the analysis may indeed be so great as to prevent the synthesis; we may so entirely pass to the suggested object, that our pleasure will be embodied in the memory of that, while the suggestive sensation will be overlooked, and the expressiveness of the present object will fail to make it beautiful. Thus the mementos of a lost friend do not become beautiful by virtue of the sentimental associations which may make them precious. The value is confined to the images of the memory; they are too clear to let any of that value escape and diffuse itself over the rest of our consciousness, and beautify the objects which we actually behold. We say explicitly: I value this trifle for its associations. And so long as this division continues, the worth of the thing is not for us æsthetic.

But a little dimming of our memory will often make it so. Let the images of the past fade, let them remain simply as a halo and suggestion of happiness hanging about a scene; then this scene, however empty and uninteresting in itself, will have a deep and intimate charm; we shall be pleased by its very vulgarity. We shall not confess so readily that we value the place for its associations; we shall rather say: I am fond of this landscape; it has for me an ineffable attraction. The treasures of the memory have been melted and dissolved, and are now gilding the object that supplants them; they are giving this object expression.

Expression then differs from material or formal value only as habit differs from instinct—in its origin. Physiologically, they are both pleasurable radiations of a given stimulus; mentally, they are both values incorporated in an object. But an observer, looking at the mind historically, sees in the one case the survival of an experience, in the other the reaction of an innate disposition. This experience, moreover, is generally rememberable, and then the extrinsic source of the charm which expression gives becomes evident even to the consciousness in which it arises. A word, for instance, is often beautiful simply by virtue of its meaning and associations; but sometimes this expressive beauty is added to a musical quality in the world itself. In all expression we may thus distinguish two terms: the first is the object actually presented, the word, the image, the expressive thing; the second is the object suggested, the further thought, emotion, or image evoked, the thing expressed.

These lie together in the mind, and their union constitutes expression. If the value lies wholly in the first term, we have no beauty of expression. The decorative inscriptions in Saracenic monuments can have no beauty of expression for one who does not read Arabic; their charm is wholly one of material and form. Or if they have any expression, it is by virtue of such thoughts as they might suggest, as, for instance, of the piety and oriental sententiousness of the builders and of the aloofness from us of all their world. And even these suggestions, being a wandering of our fancy rather than a study of the object, would fail to arouse a pleasure which would be incorporated in the present image. The scroll would remain without expression, although its presence might have suggested to us interesting visions of other things. The two terms would be too independent, and the intrinsic values of each would remain distinct from that of the other. There would be no visible expressiveness, although there might have been discursive suggestions.

Indeed, if expression were constituted by the external relation of object with object, everything would be expressive equally, indeterminately, and universally. The flower in the crannied wall would express the same thing as the bust of Cæsar or the *Critique of Pure Reason*. What constitutes the individual expressiveness of these things is the circle of thoughts allied to each in a given mind; my words, for instance, express the thoughts which they actually arouse in the reader; they may express more to one man than to another, and to me they may have expressed more or less than to you. My thoughts remain unexpressed, if my words do not arouse them in you, and very likely your greater wisdom will find in what I say the manifestation of a thousand principles of which I never dreamed. Expression depends upon the union of two terms, one of which must be furnished by the imagination; and a mind cannot furnish what it does not possess. The expressiveness of everything accordingly increases with the intelligence of the observer.

But for expression to be an element of beauty, it must, of course, fulfil another condition. I may see the relations of an object, I may understand it perfectly, and may nevertheless regard it with entire indifference. If the pleasure fails, the very substance and protoplasm of beauty is wanting. Nor, as we have seen, is even the pleasure enough; for I may receive a letter full of the most joyous news, but neither the paper, nor the writing, nor the style, need seem beautiful to me. Not until I confound the impressions, and suffuse the symbols themselves with the emotions they arouse, and find joy and sweetness in the very words I hear, will the expressiveness constitute a beauty; as when they sing, *Gloria in excelsis Deo*.

The value of the second term must be incorporated in the first; for the beauty of expression is as inherent in the object as that of material or form, only it accrues to that object not from the bare act of perception, but from the association with it of further processes, due to the existence of former impressions. We may conveniently use the word "expressiveness" to mean all the capacity of suggestion possessed by a thing, and the word "expression" for the æsthetic modification which that expressiveness may cause in it. Expressiveness is thus the power given by experience to any image to call up others in the mind; and this expressiveness becomes an æsthetic value, that is, becomes expression, when the value involved in the associations thus awakened are incorporated in the present object.

§ 49. THE ASSOCIATIVE PROCESS. The purest case in which an expressive value could arise might seem to be that in which both terms were indifferent in themselves, and what pleased was the activity of relating them. We have such a phenomenon in mathematics, and in any riddle, puzzle, or play with symbols. But such pleasures fall without the æsthetic field in the absence of any objectification; they are pleasures of exercise, and the objects involved are not regarded as the substances in which those values inhere. We think of more or less interesting problems or calculations, but it never occurs to the mathematician to establish a hierarchy of forms according to their beauty. Only by a metaphor could he say that $(a + b)^2 = a^2 + 2ab + b^2$ was a more beautiful formula than $2 + 2 = 4$. Yet in proportion as such conceptions become definite and objective in the mind, they approach æsthetic values, and the use of æsthetic epithets in describing them becomes more constant and literal.

The beauties of abstract music are but one step beyond such

mathematical relations—they are those relations presented in a sensible form, and constituting an imaginable object. But, as we see clearly in this last case, when the relation and not the terms constitute the object, we have, if there is beauty at all, a beauty of form, not of expression; for the more mathematical the charm of music is, the more form and the less expression do we see in it. In fact, the sense of relation is here the essence of the object itself, and the activity of passing from term to term, far from taking us beyond our presentation to something extrinsic, constitutes that presentation. The pleasure of this relational activity is therefore the pleasure of conceiving a determined form, and nothing could be more thoroughly a formal beauty.

And we may here insist upon a point of fundamental importance; namely, that the process of association enters consciousness as directly, and produces as simple a sensation, as any process in any organ. The pleasures and pains of cerebration, the delight and the fatigue of it, are felt exactly like bodily impressions; they have the same directness, although not the same localization. Their seat is not open to our daily observation, and therefore we leave them disembodied, and fancy they are peculiarly spiritual and intimate to the soul. Or we try to think that they flow by some logical necessity from the essences of objects simultaneously in our mind. We involve ourselves in endless perplexities in trying to deduce excellence and beauty, unity and necessity, from the describable qualities of things; we repeat the rationalistic fiction of turning the notions which we abstract from the observation of facts into the powers that give those facts character and being.

We have, for instance, in the presence of two images a sense of their incongruity; and we say that the character of the images causes this emotion; whereas in dreams we constantly have the most rapid transformations and patent contradictions without any sense of incongruity at all; because the brain is dozing and the necessary shock and mental inhibition are avoided. Add this stimulation, and the incongruity returns. Had such a shock never been felt, we should not know what incongruity meant; no more than without eyes we should know the meaning of blue or yellow.

In saying this, we are not really leaning upon physiological theory. The appeal to our knowledge of the brain facilitates the conception of the immediacy of our feelings of relation; but the immediacy would be apparent to a sharp introspection. We do not need to think of the eye or skin to feel that light and heat are ultimate data; no more do we need to think of cerebral excitements to see that right and left, before and after, good and bad, one and two, like and unlike, are irreducible feelings. The categories are senses without organs, or with organs unknown. Just as the discrimination of our feelings of colour and sound might never have been distinct and constant, had we not come upon the organs that seem to convey and control them; so perhaps our classification of our inner sensations will never be settled until their respective organs are discovered; for psychology has always been physiological, without knowing it. But this truth remains—quite apart from physical conceptions, not to speak of metaphysical materialism—that whatever the historical conditions of any state of mind may be said to be, it exists, when it does exist, immediately and absolutely; each of its distinguishable parts might conceivably have been absent from it; and its character, as well as its existence, is a mere datum of sense.

The pleasure that belongs to the consciousness of relations is therefore as immediate as any other; indeed, our emotional consciousness is always single, but we treat it as a resultant of many and even of conflicting feelings because we look at it historically with a view to comprehending it, and distribute it into as many factors as we find objects or causes to which to attribute it. The pleasure of association is an immediate feeling, which we account for by its relation to a feeling in the past, or to cerebral structure modified by a former experience; just as memory itself, which we explain by a reference to the past, is a peculiar complication of present consciousness.

§ 50. Kinds of value in the second term. These reflections may make less surprising to us what is the most striking fact about the philosophy of expression; namely, that the value acquired by the expressive thing is often of an entirely different kind from that which the thing expressed possesses. The expression of physical pleasure, of passion, or even of pain, may constitute beauty and please the beholder. Thus the value of the second term may be physical, or practical, or even negative; and it may be transmuted, as it passes to the first term, into a value at once positive and æsthetic. The transformation of practical values into æsthetic has often been noted, and has even led to the theory that beauty is utility seen at arm's length; a premonition of pleasure and prosperity, much as smell is a premonition of taste. The transformation of negative values into positive has naturally attracted even more attention, and given rise to various theories of the comic, tragic, and sublime. For these three species of æsthetic good seem to please us by the suggestion of evil; and the problem arises how a mind can be made happier by having suggestions of unhappiness stirred within it; an unhappiness it cannot understand without in some degree sharing in it. We must now turn to the analysis of this question.

The expressiveness of a smile is not discovered exactly through association of images. The child smiles (without knowing it) when he feels pleasure; and the nurse smiles back; his own pleasure is associated with her conduct, and her smile is therefore expressive of pleasure. The fact of his pleasure at her smile is the ground of his instinctive belief in her pleasure in it. For this reason the circumstances expressive of happiness are not those that are favourable to it in reality, but those that are congruous with it in idea. The green of spring, the bloom of youth, the variability of childhood, the splendour of wealth and beauty, all these are symbols of happiness, not because they have been known to accompany it in fact,—for they do not, any more than their opposites,—but because they produce an image and echo of it in us æsthetically. We believe those things to be happy which it makes us happy to think of or to see; the belief in the blessedness of the supreme being itself has no other foundation. Our joy in the thought of omniscience makes us attribute joy to the possession of it, which it would in fact perhaps be very far from involving or even allowing.

The expressiveness of forms has a value as a sign of the life that actually inhabits those forms only when they resemble our own body; it is then probable that similar conditions of body involve, in them and in us, similar emotions; and we should not long continue to regard as the expression of pleasure an attitude that we know, by experience in our own person, to accompany pain. Children, indeed, may innocently torture animals, not having enough sense of analogy to be stopped by the painful suggestions of their writhings; and, although in a rough way we soon correct these crying misinterpretations by a better classification of experience, we nevertheless remain essentially subject to the same error. We cannot escape it, because the method which involves it is the only one that justifies belief in objective consciousness at all. Analogy of bodies helps us to distribute and classify the life we conceive about us; but what leads us to conceive it is the direct association of our own feeling with images of things, an association which precedes any clear representation of our own gestures and attitude. I know that smiles mean pleasure before I have caught myself smiling in the glass; they mean pleasure because they give it.

Since these æsthetic effects include some of the most moving and profound beauties, philosophers have not been slow to turn the unanalyzed paradox of their formation into a principle, and to explain by it the presence and necessity of evil. As in the tragic and the sublime, they have thought, the sufferings and dangers to which a hero is exposed seem to add to his virtue and dignity, and to our sacred joy in the contemplation of him, so the sundry evils of life may be elements in the transcendent glory of the whole. And once fired by this thought, those who pretend to justify the ways of God to man have, naturally, not stopped to consider whether so edifying a phenomenon was not a hasty illusion. They have, indeed, detested any attempt to explain it rationally, as tending to obscure one of the moral laws of the universe. In venturing, therefore, to repeat such an attempt, we should not be too sanguine of success; for we have to encounter not only the intrinsic difficulties of the problem, but also a wide-spread and arrogant metaphysical prejudice.

For the sake of greater clearness we may begin by classifying the values that can enter into expression; we shall then be better able to judge by what combinations of them various well-known effects and emotions are produced. The intrinsic value of the first term can be entirely neglected, since it does not contribute to expression. It does, however, contribute greatly to the beauty of the expressive object. The first term is the source of stimulation, and the acuteness and pleasantness of this determine to a great extent the character and sweep of the associations that will be aroused. Very often the pleasantness of the medium will counterbalance the disagreeableness of the import, and expressions, in themselves hideous or inappropriate, may be excused for the sake of the object that conveys them. A beautiful voice will redeem a vulgar song, a beautiful colour and texture an unmeaning composition. Beauty in the first term—beauty of sound, rhythm, and image—will make any thought whatever poetic, while no thought whatever can be so without that immediate beauty of presentation.[1]

---

[1] Curiously enough, common speech here reverses our use of terms, because it looks at the matter from the practical instead of from the æsthetic point of view, regarding (very unpsychologically) the thought as the source of the image, not the image as the source of the thought. People call the words the expression of the thought: whereas for the observer, the hearer (and generally for the speaker, too), the words are the datum and the thought is their expressiveness—that which they suggest.

§ 51. ÆSTHETIC VALUE IN THE SECOND TERM. That the noble associations of any object should embellish that object is very comprehensible. Homer furnishes us with a good illustration of the constant employment of this effect. The first term, one need hardly say, leaves with him little to be desired. The verse is beautiful. Sounds, images, and composition conspire to stimulate and delight. This immediate beauty is sometimes used to clothe things terrible and sad; there is no dearth of the tragic in Homer. But the tendency of his poetry is nevertheless to fill the outskirts of our consciousness with the trooping images of things no less fair and noble than the verse itself. The heroes are virtuous. There is none of importance who is not admirable in his way. The palaces, the arms, the horses, the sacrifices, are always excellent. The women are always stately and beautiful. The ancestry and the history of every one are honourable and good. The whole Homeric world is clean, clear, beautiful, and providential, and no small part of the perennial charm of the poet is that he thus immerses us in an atmosphere of beauty; a beauty not concentrated and reserved for some extraordinary sentiment, action, or person, but permeating the whole and colouring the common world of soldiers and sailors, war and craft, with a marvellous freshness and inward glow. There is nothing in the associations of life in this world or in another to contradict or disturb our delight. All is beautiful, and beautiful through and through.

Something of this quality meets us in all simple and idyllic compositions. There is, for instance, a popular demand that stories and comedies should "end well." The hero and heroine must be young and handsome; unless they die,—which is another matter,—they must not in the end be poor. The landscape in the play must be beautiful; the dresses pretty; the plot without serious mishap. A pervasive presentation of pleasure must give warmth and ideality to the whole. In the proprieties of social life we find the same principle; we study to make our surroundings, manner, and conversation suggest nothing but what is pleasing. We hide the ugly and disagreeable portion of our lives, and do not allow the least hint of it to come to light upon festive and public occasions. Whenever, in a word, a thoroughly pleasing effect is found, it is found by the expression, as well as presentation, of what is in itself pleasing—and when this effect is to be produced artificially, we attain it by the suppression of all expression that is not suggestive of something good.

If our consciousness were exclusively æsthetic, this kind of expression would be the only one allowed in art or prized in nature. We should avoid as a shock or an insipidity, the suggestion of anything not intrinsically beautiful. As there would be no values not æsthetic, our pleasure could never be heightened by any other kind of interest. But as contemplation is actually a luxury in our lives, and things interest us chiefly on passionate and practical grounds, the accumulation of values too exclusively æsthetic produces in our minds an effect of closeness and artificiality. So selective a diet cloys, and our palate, accustomed to much daily vinegar and salt, is surfeited by such unmixed sweet.

Instead we prefer to see through the medium of art—through the beautiful first term of our expression—the miscellaneous world which is so well known to us—perhaps so dear, and at any rate so inevitable, an object. We are more thankful for this presentation of the unlovely truth in a lovely form, than for the like presentation of an abstract beauty; what is lost in the purity of the pleasure is gained in the stimulation of our attention, and in the relief of viewing with æsthetic detachment the same things that in practical life hold tyrannous dominion over our souls. The beauty that is associated only with other beauty is therefore a sort of æsthetic dainty; it leads the fancy through a fairyland of lovely forms, where we must forget the common objects of our interest. The charm of such an idealization is undeniable; but the other important elements of our memory and will cannot long be banished. Thoughts of labour, ambition, lust, anger, confusion, sorrow, and death must needs mix with our contemplation and lend their various expressions to the objects with which in experience they are so closely allied. Hence the incorporation in the beautiful of values of other sorts, and the comparative rareness in nature or art of expressions the second term of which has only æsthetic value.

§ 52. Practical value in the same. More important and frequent is the case of the expression of utility. This is found whenever the second term is the idea of something of practical advantage to us, the premonition of which brings satisfaction; and this satisfaction prompts an approval of the presented object. The tone of our consciousness is raised by the foretaste of a success; and this heightened pleasure is objectified in the present image, since the associated image to which the satisfaction properly belongs often fails to become distinct. We do not conceive clearly what this practical advantage will be; but the vague sense that an advantage is there, that something desirable has been done, accompanies the presentation, and gives it expression.

The case that most resembles that of which we have been just speaking, is perhaps that in which the second term is a piece of interesting information, a theory, or other intellectual datum. Our interest in facts and theories, when not æsthetic, is of course practical; it consists in their connexion with our interests, and in the service they can render us in the execution of our designs. Intellectual values are utilitarian in their origin but æsthetic in their form, since the advantage of knowledge is often lost sight of, and ideas are prized for their own sake. Curiosity can become a disinterested passion, and yield intimate and immediate satisfaction like any other impulse.

When we have before us, for instance, a fine map, in which the line of coast, now rocky, now sandy, is clearly indicated, together with the windings of the rivers, the elevations of the land, and the distribution of the population, we have the simultaneous suggestion of so many facts, the sense of mastery over so much reality, that we gaze at it with delight, and need no practical motive to keep us studying it, perhaps for hours together. A map is not naturally thought of as an æsthetic object; it is too exclusively expressive. The first term is passed over as a mere symbol, and the mind is filled either with imaginations of the landscape the country would really offer, or with thoughts about its history and inhabitants. These circumstances prevent the ready objectification of our pleasure in the map itself. And yet, let the tints of it be a little subtle, let the lines be a little delicate, and the masses of land and sea somewhat balanced, and we really have a beautiful thing; a thing the charm of which consists almost entirely in its meaning, but which nevertheless pleases us in the same way as a picture or a graphic symbol might please. Give the symbol a little intrinsic worth of form, line, and colour, and it attracts like a magnet all the values of the things it is known to symbolize. It becomes beautiful in its expressiveness.

Hardly different from this example is that of travel or of reading; for in these employments we get many æsthetic pleasures, the origin of which is in the satisfaction of curiosity and intelligence. When we say admiringly of anything that it is characteristic, that it embodies a whole period or a whole man, we are absorbed by the pleasant sense that it offers innumerable avenues of approach to interesting and important things. The less we are able to specify what these are, the more beautiful will the object be that expresses them. For if we could specify them, the felt value would disintegrate, and distribute itself among the ideas of the suggested things, leaving the expressive object bare of all interest, like the letters of a printed page.

The courtiers of Philip the Second probably did not regard his rooms at the Escurial as particularly interesting, but simply as small, ugly, and damp. The character which we find in them and which makes us regard them as eminently expressive of whatever was sinister in the man, probably did not strike them. They knew the king, and had before them words, gestures, and acts enough in which to read his character. But all these living facts are wanting to our experience; and it is the suggestion of them in their unrealizable vagueness that fills the apartments of the monarch with such pungent expression. It is not otherwise with all emphatic expressiveness—moonlight and castle moats, minarets and cypresses, camels filing through the desert—such images get their character from the strong but misty atmosphere of sentiment and adventure which clings about them. The profit of travel, and the extraordinary charm of all visible relics of antiquity, consists in the acquisition of images in which to focus a mass of discursive knowledge, not otherwise felt together. Such images are concrete symbols of much latent experience, and the deep roots of association give them the same hold upon our attention which might be secured by a fortunate form or splendid material.

§ 53. Cost as an element of effect. There is one consideration which often adds much to the interest with which we view an object, but which we might be virtuously inclined not to admit among æsthetic values. I mean cost. Cost is practical value expressed in abstract terms, and from the price of anything we can often infer what relation it has to the desires and efforts of mankind. There is no reason why cost, or the circumstances which are its basis, should not, like other practical values, heighten the tone of consciousness, and add to the pleasure with which we view an object. In fact, such is our daily experience; for great as is the sensuous beauty of gems, their rarity and price adds an expression of distinction to them, which they would never have if they were cheap.

The circumstance that makes the appreciation of cost often unæsthetic is the abstractness of that quality. The price of an object is an algebraic symbol, it is a conventional term, invented to facilitate our operations, which remains arid and unmeaning if we stop with it and forget to translate it again at the end into its concrete equivalent. The commercial mind dwells in that intermediate limbo of symbolized values; the calculator's senses are muffled by his intellect and by his habit of abbreviated thinking. His mental process is a reckoning that loses sight of its original values, and is over without reaching any concrete image. Therefore the knowledge of cost, when expressed in terms of money, is incapable of contributing to æsthetic effect, but the reason is not so much that the suggested value is not æsthetic, as that no real value is suggested at all. No object of any kind is presented to the mind by the numerical expression. If we reinterpret our price, however, and translate it back into the facts which constitute it, into the materials employed, their original place and quality, and the labour and art which transformed them into the present thing, then we add to the æsthetic value of the object, by the expression which we find in it, not of its price in money, but of its human cost. We have now the consciousness of the real values which it represents, and these values, sympathetically present to the fancy, increase our present interest and admiration.

I believe economists count among the elements of the value of an object the rarity of its material, the labour of its manufacture, and the distance from which it is brought. Now all these qualities, if attended to in themselves, appeal greatly to the imagination. We have a natural interest in what is rare and affects us with unusual sensations. What comes from a far country carries our thoughts there, and gains by the wealth and picturesqueness of its associations. And that on which human labour has been spent, especially if it was a labour of love, and is apparent in the product, has one of the deepest possible claims to admiration. So that the standard of cost, the most vulgar of all standards, is such only when it remains empty and abstract. Let the thoughts wander back and consider the elements of value, and our appreciation, from being verbal and commercial, becomes poetic and real.

We have in this one more example of the manner in which practical values, when suggested by and incorporated in any object, contribute to its beauty. Our sense of what lies behind, unlovely though that background may be, gives interest and poignancy to that which is present; our attention and wonder are engaged, and a new meaning and importance is added to such intrinsic beauty as the presentation may possess.

§ 54. THE EXPRESSION OF ECONOMY AND FITNESS. The same principle explains the effect of evident cleanliness, security, economy, and comfort. This Dutch charm hardly needs explanation; we are conscious of the domesticity and neatness which pleases us in it. There are few things more utterly discomforting to our minds than waste: it is a sort of pungent extract and quintessence of folly. The visible manifestation of it is therefore very offensive; and that of its absence very reassuring. The force of our approval of practical fitness and economy in things rises into an appreciation that is half-æsthetic, and which becomes wholly so when the fit form becomes fixed in a type, to the lines of which we are accustomed; so that the practical necessity of the form is heightened and concentrated into the æsthetic propriety of it.

The much-praised expression of function and truth in architectural works reduces itself to this principle. The useful contrivance at first appeals to our practical approval; while we admire its ingenuity, we cannot fail to become gradually accustomed to its presence, and to register with attentive pleasure the relation of its parts. Utility, as we have pointed out in its place, is thus the guiding principle in the determination of forms.

The recurring observation of the utility, economy, and fitness of the traditional arrangement in buildings or other products of art, re-enforces this formal expectation with a reflective approval. We are accustomed, for instance, to sloping roofs; the fact that they were necessary has made them familiar, and the fact that they are familiar has made them objects of study and of artistic enjoyment. If at any moment, however, the notion of condemning them passes through the mind,—if we have visions of the balustrade against the sky,—we revert to our homely image with kindly loyalty, when we remember the long months of rain and snow, and the comfortless leaks to be avoided. The thought of a glaring, practical unfitness is enough to spoil our pleasure in any form, however beautiful intrinsically, while the sense of practical fitness is enough to reconcile us to the most awkward and rude contrivances.

This principle is, indeed, not a fundamental, but an auxiliary one; the expression of utility modifies effect, but does not constitute it. There would be a kind of superstitious haste in the notion that what is convenient and economical is necessarily and by miracle beautiful. The uses and habits of one place and society require works which are or may easily become intrinsically beautiful; the uses and habits of another make these beautiful works impossible. The beauty has a material and formal basis that we have already studied; no fitness of design will make a building of ten equal storeys as beautiful as a pavilion or a finely proportioned tower; no utility will make a steamboat as beautiful as a sailing vessel. But the forms once established, with their various intrinsic characters, the fitness we know to exist in them will lend them some added charm, or their unfitness will disquiet us, and haunt us like a conscientious qualm. The other interests of our lives here mingle with the purely æsthetic, to enrich or to embitter it.

If Sybaris is so sad a name to the memory—and who is without some Sybaris of his own?—if the image of it is so tormenting and in the end so disgusting, this is not because we no longer think its marbles bright, its fountains cool, its athletes strong, or its roses fragrant; but because, mingled with all these supreme beauties, there is the ubiquitous shade of Nemesis, the sense of a vacant will and a suicidal inhumanity. The intolerableness of this moral condition poisons the beauty which continues to be felt. If this beauty did not exist, and was not still desired, the tragedy would disappear and Jehovah would be deprived of the worth of his victim. The sternness of moral forces lies precisely in this, that the sacrifices morality imposes upon us are real, that the things it renders impossible are still precious.

We are accustomed to think of prudence as estranging us only from low and ignoble things; we forget that utility and the need of system in our lives is a bar also to the free flights of the spirit. The highest instincts tend to disorganization as much as the lowest, since order and benefit is what practical morality everywhere insists upon, while sanctity and genius are as rebellious as vice. The constant demands of the heart and the belly can allow man only an incidental indulgence in the pleasures of the eye and the understanding. For this reason, utility keeps close watch over beauty, lest in her wilfulness and riot she should offend against our practical needs and ultimate happiness. And when the conscience is keen, this vigilance of the practical imagination over the speculative ceases to appear as an eventual and external check. The least suspicion of luxury, waste, impurity, or cruelty is then a signal for alarm and insurrection. That which emits this *sapor hœreticus* becomes so initially horrible, that naturally no beauty can ever be discovered in it; the senses and imagination are in that case inhibited by the conscience.

For this reason, the doctrine that beauty is essentially nothing but the expression of moral or practical good appeals to persons of predominant moral sensitiveness, not only because they wish it were the truth, but because it largely describes the experience of their own minds, somewhat warped in this particular. It will further be observed that the moralists are much more able to condemn than to appreciate the effects of the arts. Their taste is delicate without being keen, for the principle on which they judge is one which really operates to control and extend æsthetic effects; it is a source of expression and of certain *nuances* of satisfaction; but it is foreign to the stronger and more primitive æsthetic values to which the same persons are comparatively blind.

§ 55. The authority of morals over æsthetics. The extent to which æsthetic goods should be sacrificed is, of course, a moral question; for the function of practical reason is to compare, combine, and harmonize all our interests, with a view to attaining the greatest satisfactions of which our nature is capable. We must expect, therefore, that virtue should place the same restraint upon all our passions—not from superstitious aversion to any one need, but from an equal concern for them all. The consideration to be given to our æsthetic pleasures will depend upon their greater or less influence upon our happiness; and as this influence varies in different ages and countries, and with different individuals, it will be right to let æsthetic demands count for more or for less in the organization of life.

We may, indeed, according to our personal sympathies, prefer one type of creature to another. We may love the martial, or the angelic, or the political temperament. We may delight to find in others that balance of susceptibilities and enthusiasms which we feel in our own breast. But no moral precept can require one species or individual to change its nature in order to resemble another, since such a requirement can have no power or authority over those on whom we would impose it. All that morality can require is the inward harmony of each life: and if we still abhor the thought of a possible being who should be happy without love, or knowledge, or beauty, the aversion we feel is not moral but instinctive, not rational but human. What revolts us is not the want of excellence in that other creature, but his want of affinity to ourselves. Could we survey the whole universe, we might indeed assign to each species a moral dignity proportionate to its general beneficence and inward wealth; but such an absolute standard, if it exists, is incommunicable to us; and we are reduced to judging of the excellence of every nature by its relation to the human.

All these matters, however, belong to the sphere of ethics, nor should we give them here even a passing notice, but for the influence which moral ideas exert over æsthetic judgments. Our sense of practical benefit not only determines the moral value of beauty, but sometimes even its existence as an æsthetic good. Especially in the right *selection* of effects, these considerations have weight. Forms in themselves pleasing may become disagreeable when the practical interests then uppermost in the mind cannot, without violence, yield a place to them. Thus too much eloquence in a diplomatic document, or in a familiar letter, or in a prayer, is an offence not only against practical sense, but also against taste. The occasion has tuned us to a certain key of sentiment, and deprived us of the power to respond to other stimuli.

If things of moment are before us, we cannot stop to play with symbols and figures of speech. We cannot attend to them with pleasure, and therefore they lose the beauty they might elsewhere have had. They are offensive, not in themselves,—for nothing is intrinsically ugly,—but by virtue of our present demand for something different. A prison as gay as a bazaar, a church as dumb as a prison, offend by their failure to support by their æsthetic quality the moral emotion with which we approach them. The arts must study their occasions; they must stand modestly aside until they can slip in fitly into the interstices of life. This is the consequence of the superficial stratum on which they flourish; their roots, as we have seen, are not deep in the world, and they appear only as unstable, superadded activities, employments of our freedom, after the work of life is done and the terror of it is allayed. They must, therefore, fit their forms, like parasites, to the stouter growths to which they cling.

Herein lies the greatest difficulty and nicety of art. It must not only create things abstractly beautiful, but it must conciliate all the competitors these may have to the attention of the world, and must know how to insinuate their charms among the objects of our passion. But this subserviency and enforced humility of beauty is not without its virtue and reward. If the æsthetic habit lie under the necessity of respecting and observing our passions, it possesses the privilege of soothing our griefs. There is no situation so terrible that it may not be relieved by the momentary pause of the mind to contemplate it æsthetically.

Grief itself becomes in this way not wholly pain; a sweetness is added to it by our reflection. The saddest scenes may lose their bitterness in their beauty. This ministration makes, as it were, the piety of the Muses, who succour their mother, Life, and repay her for their nurture by the comfort of their continual presence. The æsthetic world is limited in its scope; it must submit to the control of the organizing reason, and not trespass upon more useful and holy ground. The garden must not encroach upon the corn-fields; but the eye of the gardener may transform the corn-fields themselves by dint of loving observation into a garden of a soberer kind. By finding grandeur in our disasters, and merriment in our mishaps, the æsthetic sense thus mollifies both, and consoles us for the frequent impossibility of a serious and perfect beauty.

§ 56. NEGATIVE VALUES IN THE SECOND TERM. All subjects, even the most repellent, when the circumstances of life thrust them before us, can thus be observed with curiosity and treated with art. The calling forth of these æsthetic functions softens the violence of our sympathetic reaction. If death, for instance, did not exist and did not thrust itself upon our thoughts with painful importunity, art would never have been called upon to soften and dignify it, by presenting it in beautiful forms and surrounding it with consoling associations. Art does not seek out the pathetic, the tragic, and the absurd; it is life that has imposed them upon our attention, and enlisted art in their service, to make the contemplation of them, since it is inevitable, at least as tolerable as possible.

The agreeableness of the presentation is thus mixed with the horror of the thing; and the result is that while we are saddened by the truth we are delighted by the vehicle that conveys it to us. The mixture of these emotions constitutes the peculiar flavour and poignancy of pathos. But because unlovely objects and feelings are often so familiar as to be indifferent or so momentous as to be alone in the mind, we are led into the confusion of supposing that beauty depends upon them for its æsthetic value; whereas the truth is that only by the addition of positive beauties can these evil experiences be made agreeable to contemplation.

There is, in reality, no such paradox in the tragic, comic, and sublime, as has been sometimes supposed. We are not pleased by virtue of the suggested evils, but in spite of them; and if ever the charm of the beautiful presentation sinks so low, or the vividness of the represented evil rises so high, that the balance is in favour of pain, at that very moment the whole object becomes horrible, passes out of the domain of art, and can be justified only by its scientific or moral uses. As an æsthetic value it is destroyed; it ceases to be a benefit; and the author of it, if he were not made harmless by the neglect that must soon overtake him, would have to be punished as a malefactor who adds to the burden of mortal life. For the sad, the ridiculous, the grotesque, and the terrible, unless they become æsthetic goods, remain moral evils.

We have, therefore, to study the various æsthetic, intellectual, and moral compensations by which the mind can be brought to contemplate with pleasure a thing which, if experienced alone, would be the cause of pain. There is, to be sure, a way of avoiding this inquiry. We might assert that since all moderate excitement is pleasant, there is nothing strange in the fact that the representation of evil should please; for the experience is evil by virtue of the pain it gives; but it gives pain only when felt with great intensity. Observed from afar, it is a pleasing impression; it is vivid enough to interest, but not acute enough to wound. This simple explanation is possible in all those cases where æsthetic effect is gained by the inhibition of sympathy.

The term "evil" is often a conventional epithet; a conflagration may be called an evil, because it usually involves loss and suffering; but if, without caring for a loss and suffering we do not share, we are delighted by the blaze, and still say that what pleases us is an evil, we are using this word as a conventional appellation, not as the mark of a felt value. We are not pleased by an evil; we are pleased by a vivid and exciting sensation, which is a good, but which has for objective cause an event which may indeed be an evil to others, but about the consequences of which we are not thinking at all. There is, in this sense, nothing in all nature, perhaps, which is not an evil; nothing which is not unfavourable to some interest, and does not involve some infinitesimal or ultimate suffering in the universe of life.

But when we are ignorant or thoughtless, this suffering is to us as if it did not exist. The pleasures of drinking and walking are not tragic to us, because we may be poisoning some bacillus or crushing some worm. To an omniscient intelligence such acts may be tragic by virtue of the insight into their relations to conflicting impulses; but unless these impulses are present to the same mind, there is no consciousness of tragedy. The child that, without understanding of the calamity, should watch a shipwreck from the shore, would have a simple emotion of pleasure as from a jumping jack; what passes for tragic interest is often nothing but this. If he understood the event, but was entirely without sympathy, he would have the æsthetic emotion of the careless tyrant, to whom the notion of suffering is no hindrance to the enjoyment of the lyre. If the temper of his tyranny were purposely cruel, he might add to that æsthetic delight the luxury of *Schadenfreude;* but the pathos and horror of the sight could only appeal to a man who realized and shared the sufferings he beheld.

A great deal of brutal tragedy has been endured in the world because the rudeness of the representation, or of the public, or of both, did not allow a really sympathetic reaction to arise. We all smile when Punch beats Judy in the puppet show. The treatment and not the subject is what makes a tragedy. A parody of *Hamlet* or of *King Lear* would not be a tragedy; and these tragedies themselves are not wholly such, but by the strain of wit and nonsense they contain are, as it were, occasional parodies on themselves. By treating a tragic subject bombastically or satirically we can turn it into an amusement for the public; they will not feel the griefs which we have been careful to harden them against by arousing in them contrary emotions. A work, nominally a work of art, may also appeal to non-æsthetic feelings by its political bias, brutality, or obscenity. But if an effect of true pathos is sought, the sympathy of the observer must be aroused; we must awaken in him the emotion we describe. The intensity of the impression must not be so slight that its painful quality is not felt; for it is this very sense of pain, mingling with the æsthetic excitement of the spectacle, that gives it a tragic or pathetic colouring.

We cannot therefore rest in the assertion that the slighter degree of excitement is pleasant, when a greater degree of the same would be disagreeable; for that principle does not express the essence of the matter, which is that we must be aware of the evil, and conscious of it as such, absorbed more or less in the experience of the sufferer, and consequently suffering ourselves, before we can experience the essence of tragic emotion. This emotion must therefore be complex; it must contain an element of pain overbalanced by an element of pleasure; in our delight there must be a distinguishable touch of shrinking and sorrow; for it is this conflict and rending of our will, this fascination by what is intrinsically terrible or sad, that gives these turbid feelings their depth and pungency.

§ 57. INFLUENCE OF THE FIRST TERM IN THE PLEASING EXPRESSION OF EVIL. A striking proof of the compound nature of tragic effects can be given by a simple experiment. Remove from any drama—say from *Othello*—the charm of the medium of presentation; reduce the tragedy to a mere account of the facts and of the words spoken, such as our newspapers almost daily contain; and the tragic dignity and beauty is entirely lost. Nothing remains but a disheartening item of human folly, which may still excite curiosity, but which will rather defile than purify the mind that considers it. A French poet has said:

> Il n'est de vulgaire chagrin
> Que celui d'une âme vulgaire.

The counterpart of this maxim is equally true. There is no noble sorrow except in a noble mind, because what is noble is the reaction upon the sorrow, the attitude of the man in its presence, the language in which he clothes it, the associations with which he surrounds it, and the fine affections and impulses which shine through it. Only by suffusing some sinister experience with this moral light, as a poet may do who carries that light within him, can we raise misfortune into tragedy and make it better for us to remember our lives than to forget them.

There are times, although rare, when men are noble in the very moment of passion: when that passion is not unqualified, but already mastered by reflection and levelled with truth. Then the experience is itself the tragedy, and no poet is needed to make it beautiful in representation, since the sufferer has been an artist himself, and has moulded what he has endured. But usually these two stages have to be successive: first we suffer, afterwards we sing. An interval is necessary to make feeling presentable, and subjugate it to that form in which alone it is beautiful.

This form appeals to us in itself, and without its aid no subject-matter could become an æsthetic object. The more terrible the experience described, the more powerful must the art be which is to transform it. For this reason prose and literalness are more tolerable in comedy than in tragedy; any violent passion, any overwhelming pain, if it is not to make us think of a demonstration in pathology, and bring back the smell of ether, must be rendered in the most exalted style. Metre, rhyme, melody, the widest flights of allusion, the highest reaches of fancy, are there in place. For these enable the mind swept by the deepest cosmic harmonies, to endure and absorb the shrill notes which would be intolerable in a poorer setting.

The sensuous harmony of words, and still more the effects of rhythm, are indispensable at this height of emotion. Evolutionists have said that violent emotion naturally expresses itself in rhythm. That is hardly an empirical observation, nor can the expressiveness of rhythms be made definite enough to bear specific association with complex feelings. But the suspension and rush of sound and movement have in themselves a strong effect; we cannot undergo them without profound excitement; and this, like martial music, nerves us to courage and, by a sort of intoxication, bears us along amid scenes which might otherwise be sickening. The vile effect of literal and disjointed renderings of suffering, whether in writing or acting, proves how necessary is the musical quality to tragedy—a fact Aristotle long ago set forth. The afflatus of rhythm, even if it be the pomp of the Alexandrine, sublimates the passion, and clarifies its mutterings into poetry. This breadth and rationality are necessary to art, which is not skill merely, but skill in the service of beauty.

§ 58. Mixture of other expressions, including that of truth. To the value of these sensuous and formal elements must be added the continual suggestion of beautiful and happy things, which no tragedy is sombre enough to exclude. Even if we do not go so far as to intersperse comic scenes and phrases into a pathetic subject,—a rude device, since the comic passages themselves need that purifying which they are meant to effect,—we must at least relieve our theme with pleasing associations. For this reason we have palaces for our scene, rank, beauty, and virtue in our heroes, nobility in their passions and in their fate, and altogether a sort of glorification of life without which tragedy would lose both in depth of pathos—since things so precious are destroyed—and in subtlety of charm, since things so precious are manifested.

Indeed, one of the chief charms that tragedies have is the suggestion of what they might have been if they had not been tragedies. The happiness which glimmers through them, the hopes, loves, and ambitions of which it is made, these things fascinate us, and win our sympathy; so that we are all the more willing to suffer with our heroes, even if we are at the same time all the more sensitive to their suffering. Too wicked a character or too unrelieved a situation revolts us for this reason. We do not find enough expression of good to make us endure the expression of the evil.

A curious exception to this rule, which, however, admirably illustrates the fundamental principle of it, is where by the diversity of evils represented the mind is relieved from painful absorption in any of them. There is a scene in *King Lear,* where the horror of the storm is made to brood over at least four miseries, that of the king, of the fool, of Edgar in his real person, and of Edgar in his assumed character. The vividness of each of these portrayals, with its different note of pathos, keeps the mind detached and free, forces it to compare and reflect, and thereby to universalize the spectacle. Yet even here, the beautiful effect is not secured without some touches of good. How much is not gained by the dumb fidelity of the fool, and by the sublime humanity of Lear, when he says, "Art cold? There is a part of me is sorry for thee yet."

Yet all these compensations would probably be unavailing but for another which the saddest things often have,—the compensation of being true. Our practical and intellectual nature is deeply interested in truth. What describes fact appeals to us for that reason; it has an inalienable interest. However unpleasant truth may prove, we long to know it, partly perhaps because experience has shown us the prudence of this kind of intellectual courage, and chiefly because the consciousness of ignorance and the dread of the unknown is more tormenting than any possible discovery. A primitive instinct makes us turn the eyes full on any object that appears in the dim borderland of our field of vision—and this all the more quickly, the more terrible that object threatens to be.

This physical thirst for seeing has its intellectual extension. We covet truth, and to attain it, amid all accidents, is a supreme satisfaction. Now this satisfaction the representation of evil can also afford. Whether we hear the account of some personal accident, or listen to the symbolic representation of the inherent tragedy of life, we crave the same knowledge; the desire for truth makes us welcome eagerly whatever comes in its name. To be sure, the relief of such instruction does not of itself constitute an æsthetic pleasure: the other conditions of beauty remain to be fulfilled. But the satisfaction of so imperious an intellectual instinct insures our willing attention to the tragic object, and strengthens the hold which any beauties it may possess will take upon us. An intellectual value stands ready to be transmuted into an æsthetic one, if once its discursiveness is lost, and it is left hanging about the object as a vague sense of dignity and meaning.

To this must be added the specific pleasure of recognition, one of the keenest we have, and the sentimental one of nursing our own griefs and dignifying them by assimilation to a less inglorious representation of them. Here we have truth on a small scale; conformity in the fiction to incidents of our personal experience. Such correspondences are the basis of much popular appreciation of trivial and undigested works that appeal to some momentary phase of life or feeling, and disappear with it. They have the value of personal stimulants only; they never achieve beauty. Like the souvenirs of last season's gayeties, or the diary of an early love, they are often hideous in themselves in proportion as they are redolent with personal associations. But however hopelessly mere history or confession may fail to constitute a work of art, a work of art that has an historical warrant, either literal or symbolical, gains the support of that vivid interest we have in facts. And many tragedies and farces, that to a mind without experience of this sublunary world might seem monstrous and disgusting fictions, may come to be forgiven and even perhaps preferred over all else, when they are found to be a sketch from life.

Truth is thus the excuse which ugliness has for being. Many people, in whom the pursuit of knowledge and the indulgence in sentiment have left no room for the cultivation of the æsthetic sense, look in art rather for this expression of fact or of passion than for the revelation of beauty. They accordingly produce and admire works without intrinsic value. They employ the procedure of the fine arts without an eye to what can give pleasure in the effect. They invoke rather the *a priori* interest which men are expected to have in the subject-matter, or in the theories and moral implied in the presentation of it. Instead of using the allurements of art to inspire wisdom, they require an appreciation of wisdom to make us endure their lack of art.

Of course, the instruments of the arts are public property and any one is free to turn them to new uses. It would be an interesting development of civilization if they should now be employed only as methods of recording scientific ideas and personal confessions. But the experiment has not succeeded and can hardly succeed. There are other simpler, clearer, and more satisfying ways of expounding truth. A man who is really a student of history or philosophy will never rest with the vague and

partial oracles of poetry, not to speak of the inarticulate suggestions of the plastic arts. He will at once make for the principles
which art cannot express, even if it can embody them, and
when those principles are attained, the works of art, if they had
no other value than that of suggesting them, will lapse from
his mind. Forms will give place to formulas as hieroglyphics have
given place to the letters of the alphabet.

If, on the other hand, the primary interest is really in beauty,
and only the confusion of a moral revolution has obscured for
a while the vision of the ideal, then as the mind regains its
mastery over the world, and digests its new experience, the
imagination will again be liberated, and create its forms by its
inward affinities, leaving all the weary burden, archæological,
psychological, and ethical, to those whose business is not to delight. But the sudden inundation of science and sentiment which
has made the mind of the nineteenth century so confused, by
overloading us with materials and breaking up our habits of
apperception and our ideals, has led to an exclusive sense of the
value of expressiveness, until this has been almost identified with
beauty. This exaggeration can best prove how the expression of
truth may enter into the play of æsthetic forces, and give a value
to representations which, but for it, would be repulsive.

§ 59. THE LIBERATION OF SELF. Hitherto we have been considering those elements of a pathetic presentation which may miti-
gate our sympathetic emotion, and make it on the whole
agreeable. These consist in the intrinsic beauties of the medium
of presentation, and in the concomitant manifestation of various
goods, notably of truth. The mixture of these values is perhaps
all we have in mildly pathetic works, in the presence of which
we are tolerably aware of a sort of balance and compensation
of emotions. The sorrow and the beauty, the hopelessness and
the consolation, mingle and merge into a kind of joy which has
its poignancy, indeed, but which is far too passive and peniten-
tial to contain the louder and sublimer of our tragic moods. In
these there is a wholeness, a strength, and a rapture, which still
demands an explanation.

Where this explanation is to be found may be guessed from
the following circumstance. The pathetic is a quality of the
object, at once lovable and sad, which we accept and allow to
flow in upon the soul; but the heroic is an attitude of the will,
by which the voices of the outer world are silenced, and a
moral energy, flowing from within, is made to triumph over

them. If we fail, therefore, to discover, by analysis of the object, anything which could make it sublime, we must not be surprised at our failure. We must remember that the object is always but a portion of our consciousness: that portion which has enough coherence and articulation to be recognized as permanent and projected into the outer world. But consciousness remains one, in spite of this diversification of its content, and the object is not really independent, but is in constant relation to the rest of the mind, in the midst of which it swims like a bubble on a dark surface of water.

The æsthetic effect of objects is always due to the total emotional value of the consciousness in which they exist. We merely attribute this value to the object by a projection which is the ground of the apparent objectivity of beauty. Sometimes this value may be inherent in the process by which the object itself is perceived; then we have sensuous and formal beauty; sometimes the value may be due to the incipient formation of other ideas, which the perception of this object evokes; then we have beauty of expression. But among the ideas with which every object has relation there is one vaguest, most comprehensive, and most powerful one, namely, the idea of self. The impulses, memories, principles, and energies which we designate by that word baffle enumeration; indeed, they constantly fade and change into one another; and whether the self is anything, everything, or nothing depends on the aspect of it which we momentarily fix, and especially on the definite object with which we contrast it.

Now, it is the essential privilege of beauty to so synthesize and bring to a focus the various impulses of the self, so to suspend them to a single image, that a great peace falls upon that perturbed kingdom. In the experience of these momentary harmonies we have the basis of the enjoyment of beauty, and of all its mystical meanings. But there are always two methods of securing harmony: one is to unify all the given elements, and another is to reject and expunge all the elements that refuse to be unified. Unity by inclusion gives us the beautiful; unity by exclusion, opposition, and isolation gives us the sublime. Both are pleasures: but the pleasure of the one is warm, passive, and pervasive; that of the other cold, imperious, and keen. The one identifies us with the world, the other raises us above it.

There can be no difficulty in understanding how the expression of evil in the object may be the occasion of this heroic reaction of the soul. In the first place, the evil may be felt; but at the same time the sense that, great as it may be in itself, it cannot touch us, may stimulate extraordinarily the consciousness of our own wholeness. This is the sublimity which Lucretius calls "sweet" in the famous lines in which he so justly analyzes it. We are not pleased because another suffers an evil, but because, seeing it is an evil, we see at the same time our own immunity from it. We might soften the picture a little, and perhaps make the principle even clearer by so doing. The shipwreck observed from the shore does not leave us wholly unmoved; we suffer, also, and if possible, would help. So, too, the spectacle of the erring world must sadden the philosopher even in the Acropolis of his wisdom; he would, if it might be, descend from his meditation and teach. But those movements of sympathy are quickly inhibited by despair of success; impossibility of action is a great condition of the sublime. If we could count the stars, we should not weep before them. While we think we can change the drama of history, and of our own lives, we are not awed by our destiny. But when the evil is irreparable, when our life is lived, a strong spirit has the sublime resource of standing at bay and of surveying almost from the other world the vicissitudes of this.

The more intimate to himself the tragedy he is able to look back upon with calmness, the more sublime that calmness is, and the more divine the ecstasy in which he achieves it. For the more of the accidental vesture of life we are able to strip ourselves of, the more naked and simple is the surviving spirit; the more complete its superiority and unity, and, consequently, the more unqualified its joy. There remains little in us, then, but that intellectual essence, which several great philosophers have called eternal and identified with the Divinity.

A single illustration may help to fix these principles in the mind. When Othello has discovered his fatal error, and is resolved to take his own life, he stops his groaning, and addresses the ambassadors of Venice thus:

> Speak of me as I am: nothing extenuate,
> Nor set down aught in malice: then, must you speak
> Of one that loved, not wisely, but too well;
> Of one not easily jealous, but, being wrought,
> Perplexed in the extreme; of one whose hand,
> Like the base Indian, threw a pearl away
> Richer than all his tribe; of one whose subdued eyes,
> Albeit unusèd to the melting mood,
> Drop tears as fast as the Arabian trees
> Their medicinal gum. Set you down this:
> And say, besides, that in Aleppo once

When a malignant and a turbaned Turk
Beat a Venetian, and traduced the state,
I took by the throat the circumcisèd dog,
And smote him, thus.

There is a kind of criticism that would see in all these allusions, figures of speech, and wandering reflections, an unnatural rendering of suicide. The man, we might be told, should have muttered a few broken phrases, and killed himself without this pomp of declamation, like the jealous husbands in the daily papers. But the conventions of the tragic stage are more favourable to psychological truth than the conventions of real life. If we may trust the imagination (and in imagination lies, as we have seen, the test of propriety), this is what Othello would have felt. If he had not expressed it, his dumbness would have been due to external hindrances, not to the failure in his mind of just such complex and rhetorical thoughts as the poet has put into his mouth. The height of passion is naturally complex and rhetorical. Love makes us poets, and the approach of death should make us philosophers. When a man knows that his life is over, he can look back upon it from a universal standpoint. He has nothing more to live for, but if the energy of his mind remains unimpaired, he will still wish to live, and, being cut off from his personal ambitions, he will impute to himself a kind of vicarious immortality by identifying himself with what is eternal. He speaks of himself as he is, or rather as he was. He sums himself up, and points to his achievement. This I have been, says he, this I have done.

This comprehensive and impartial view, this synthesis and objectification of experience, constitutes the liberation of the soul and the essence of sublimity. That the hero attains it at the end consoles us, as it consoles him, for his hideous misfortunes. Our pity and terror are indeed purged; we go away knowing that, however tangled the net may be in which we feel ourselves caught, there is liberation beyond, and an ultimate peace.

§ 60. THE SUBLIME INDEPENDENT OF THE EXPRESSION OF EVIL. So natural is the relation between the vivid conception of great evils, and that self-assertion of the soul which gives the emotion of the sublime, that the sublime is often thought to depend upon the terror which these conceived evils inspire. To be sure, that terror would have to be inhibited and subdued, otherwise we should have a passion too acute to be incorporated in any object; the sublime would not appear as an æsthetic quality in things, but remain merely an emotional state in the subject. But this subdued and objectified terror is what is commonly regarded as the essence of the sublime, and so great an authority as Aristotle would seem to countenance some such definition. The usual cause of the sublime is here confused, however, with the sublime itself. The suggestion of terror makes us withdraw into ourselves: there with the supervening consciousness of safety or indifference comes a rebound, and we have that emotion of detachment and liberation in which the sublime really consists.

Thoughts and actions are properly sublime, and visible things only by analogy and suggestion when they induce a certain moral emotion; whereas beauty belongs properly to sensible things, and can be predicated of moral facts only by a figure of rhetoric. What we objectify in beauty is a sensation. What we objectify in the sublime is an act. This act is necessarily pleasant, for if it were not the sublime would be a bad quality and one we should rather never encounter in the world. The glorious joy of self-assertion in the face of an uncontrollable world is indeed so deep and entire, that it furnishes just that transcendent element of worth for which we were looking when we tried to understand how the expression of pain could sometimes please. It can please, not in itself, but because it is balanced and annulled by positive pleasures, especially by this final and victorious one of detachment. If the expression of evil seems necessary to the sublime, it is so only as a condition of this moral reaction.

We are commonly too much engrossed in objects and too little centred in ourselves and our inalienable will, to see the sublimity of a pleasing prospect. We are then enticed and flattered, and won over to a commerce with these external goods, and the consummation of our happiness would lie in the perfect comprehension and enjoyment of their nature. This is the office of art and love; and its partial fulfilment is seen in every perception of beauty. But when we are checked in this sympathetic endeavour after unity and comprehension; when we come upon a great evil or an irreconcilable power, we are driven to seek our happiness by the shorter and heroic road; then we recognize the hopeless foreignness of what lies before us, and stiffen ourselves against it. We thus for the first time reach the sense of our possible separation from our world, and of our abstract stability; and with this comes the sublime.

But although experience of evil is the commonest approach

to this attitude of mind, and we commonly become philosophers only after despairing of instinctive happiness, yet there is nothing impossible in the attainment of detachment by other channels. The immense is sublime as well as the terrible; and mere infinity of the object, like its hostile nature, can have the effect of making the mind recoil upon itself. Infinity, like hostility, removes us from things, and makes us conscious of our independence. The simultaneous view of many things, innumerable attractions felt together, produce equilibrium and indifference, as effectually as the exclusion of all. If we may call the liberation of the self by the consciousness of evil in the world, the Stoic sublime, we may assert that there is also an Epicurean sublime, which consists in liberation by equipoise. Any wide survey is sublime in that fashion. Each detail may be beautiful. We may even be ready with a passionate response to its appeal. We may think we covet every sort of pleasure, and lean to every kind of vigorous, impulsive life. But let an infinite panorama be suddenly unfolded; the will is instantly paralyzed, and the heart choked. It is impossible to desire everything at once, and when all is offered and approved, it is impossible to choose everything. In this suspense, the mind soars into a kind of heaven, benevolent but unmoved.

This is the attitude of all minds to which breadth of interest or length of years has brought balance and dignity. The sacerdotal quality of old age comes from this same sympathy in disinterestedness. Old men full of hurry and passion appear as fools, because we understand that their experience has not left enough mark upon their brain to qualify with the memory of other goods any object that may be now presented. We cannot venerate any one in whom appreciation is not divorced from desire. And this elevation and detachment of the heart need not follow upon any great disappointment; it is finest and sweetest where it is the gradual fruit of many affections now merged and mellowed into a natural piety. Indeed, we are able to frame our idea of the Deity on no other model.

When the pantheists try to conceive all the parts of nature as forming a single being, which shall contain them all and yet have absolute unity, they find themselves soon denying the existence of the world they are trying to deify; for nature, reduced to the unity it would assume in an omniscient mind, is no longer nature, but something simple and impossible, the exact opposite of the real world. Such an opposition would constitute the liberation of the divine mind from nature, and its existence as a self-conscious individual. The effort after comprehensiveness of view reduces things to unity, but this unity stands out in opposition to the manifold phenomena which it transcends, and rejects as unreal.

Now this destruction of nature, which the metaphysicians since Parmenides have so often repeated (nature nevertheless surviving still), is but a theoretical counterpart and hypostasis of what happens in every man's conscience when the comprehensiveness of his experience lifts him into thought, into abstraction. The sense of the sublime is essentially mystical: it is the transcending of distinct perception in favour of a feeling of unity and volume. So in the moral sphere, we have the mutual cancelling of the passions in the breast that includes them all, and their final subsidence beneath the glance that comprehends them. This is the Epicurean approach to detachment and perfection; it leads by systematic acceptance of instinct to the same goal which the stoic and the ascetic reach by systematic rejection of instinct. It is thus possible to be moved to that self-enfranchisement which constitutes the sublime, even when the object contains no expression of evil.

This conclusion supports that part of our definition of beauty which declares that the values beauty contains are all positive; a definition which we should have had to change if we had found that the sublime depended upon the suggestion of evil for its effect. But the sublime is not the ugly, as some descriptions of it might lead us to suppose; it is the supremely, the intoxicatingly beautiful. It is the pleasure of contemplation reaching such an intensity that it begins to lose its objectivity, and to declare itself, what it always fundamentally was, an inward passion of the soul. For while in the beautiful we find the perfection of life by sinking into the object, in the sublime we find a purer and more inalienable perfection by defying the object altogether. The surprised enlargement of vision, the sudden escape from our ordinary interests and the identification of ourselves with something permanent and superhuman, something much more abstract and inalienable than our changing personality, all this carries us away from the blurred objects before us, and raises us into a sort of ecstasy.

In the trite examples of the sublime, where we speak of the vast mass, strength, and durability of objects, or of their sinister aspect, as if we were moved by them on account of our own danger, we seem to miss the point. For the suggestion of our own danger would produce a touch of fear; it would be a practical passion, or if it could by chance be objectified enough to become æsthetic, it would merely make the object hateful and repulsive, like a mangled corpse. The object is sublime when we forget our danger, when we escape from ourselves altogether, and live as it were in the object itself, energizing in imitation of its movement, and saying, "Be thou me, impetuous one!" This passage into the object, to live its life, is indeed a characteristic of all perfect contemplation. But when in thus translating ourselves we rise and play a higher personage, feeling the exhilaration of a life freer and wilder than our own, then the experience is one of sublimity. The emotion comes not from the situation we observe, but from the powers we conceive; we fail to sympathize with the struggling sailors because we sympathize too much with the wind and waves. And this mystical cruelty can extend even to ourselves; we can so feel the fascination of the cosmic forces that engulf us as to take a fierce joy in the thought of our own destruction. We can identify ourselves with the abstractest essence of reality, and, raised to that height, despise the human accidents of our own nature. Lord, we say, though thou slay me, yet will I trust in thee. The sense of suffering disappears in the sense of life and the imagination overwhelms the understanding.

§ 61. THE COMIC. Something analogous takes place in the other spheres where an æsthetic value seems to arise out of suggestions of evil, in the comic, namely, and the grotesque. But here the translation of our sympathies is partial, and we are carried away from ourselves only to become smaller. The larger humanity, which cannot be absorbed, remains ready to contradict the absurdity of our fiction. The excellence of comedy lies in the invitation to wander along some by-path of the fancy, among scenes not essentially impossible, but not to be actually enacted by us on account of the fixed circumstances of our lives. If the picture is agreeable, we allow ourselves to dream it true. We forget its relations; we forbid the eye to wander beyond the frame of the stage, or the conventions of the fiction. We indulge an illusion which deepens our sense of the essential pleasantness of things.

So far, there is nothing in comedy that is not delightful, except, perhaps, the moment when it is over. But fiction, like all error or abstraction, is necessarily unstable; and the awakening is not always reserved for the disheartening moment at the end. Everywhere, when we are dealing with pretension or mistake, we come upon sudden and vivid contradictions; changes of view, transformations of apperception which are extremely stimulating to the imagination. We have spoken of one of these: when the sudden dissolution of our common habits of thought lifts us into a mystical contemplation, filled with the sense of the sublime; when the transformation is back to common sense and reality, and away from some fiction, we have a very different emotion. We feel cheated, relieved, abashed, or amused, in proportion as our sympathy attaches more to the point of view surrendered or to that attained.

The disintegration of mental forms and their redintegration is the life of the imagination. It is a spiritual process of birth and death, nutrition and generation. The strongest emotions accompany these changes, and vary infinitely with their variations. All the qualities of discourse, wit, eloquence, cogency, absurdity, are feelings incidental to this process, and involved in the juxtapositions, tensions, and resolutions of our ideas. Doubtless the last explanation of these things would be cerebral; but we are as yet confined to verbal descriptions and classifications of them, which are always more or less arbitrary.

The most conspicuous headings under which comic effects are gathered are perhaps incongruity and degradation. But clearly it cannot be the logical essence of incongruity or degradation that constitutes the comic; for then contradiction and deterioration would always amuse. Amusement is a much more directly physical thing. We may be amused without any idea at all, as when we are tickled, or laugh in sympathy with others by a contagious imitation of their gestures. We may be amused by the mere repetition of a thing at first not amusing. There must therefore be some nervous excitement on which the feeling of amusement directly depends, although this excitement may most often coincide with a sudden transition to an incongruous or meaner image. Nor can we suppose that particular ideational excitement to be entirely dissimilar to all others; wit is often hardly distinguishable from brilliancy, as humour from pathos. We must, therefore, be satisfied with saying vaguely that the process of ideation involves various feelings of movement and relation,—feelings capable of infinite gradation and complexity, and ranging from sublimity to tedium and from pathos to uncontrollable merriment.

Certain crude and obvious cases of the comic seem to consist of little more than a shock of surprise: a pun is a sort of jack-in-the-box, popping from nowhere into our plodding thoughts. The liveliness of the interruption, and its futility, often please;

dulce est desipere in loco; and yet those who must endure the society of inveterate jokers know how intolerable this sort of scintillation can become. There is something inherently vulgar about it; perhaps because our train of thought cannot be very entertaining in itself when we are so glad to break in upon it with irrelevant nullities. The same undertone of disgust mingles with other amusing surprises, as when a dignified personage slips and falls, or some disguise is thrown off, or those things are mentioned and described which convention ignores. The novelty and the freedom please, yet the shock often outlasts the pleasure, and we have cause to wish we had been stimulated by something which did not involve this degradation. So, also, the impossibility in plausibility which tickles the fancy in Irish bulls, and in wild exaggerations, leaves an uncomfortable impression, a certain aftertaste of foolishness.

The reason will be apparent if we stop to analyze the situation. We have a prosaic background of common sense and everyday reality; upon this background an unexpected idea suddenly impinges. But the thing is a futility. The comic accident falsifies the nature before us, starts a wrong analogy in the mind, a suggestion that cannot be carried out. In a word, we are in the presence of an absurdity; and man, being a rational animal, can like absurdity no better than he can like hunger or cold. A pinch of either may not be so bad, and he will endure it merrily enough if you repay him with abundance of warm victuals; so, too, he will play with all kinds of nonsense for the sake of laughter and good fellowship and the tickling of his fancy with a sort of caricature of thought. But the qualm remains, and the pleasure is never perfect. The same exhilaration might have come without the falsification, just as repose follows more swiftly after pleasant than after painful exertions.

Fun is a good thing, but only when it spoils nothing better. The best place for absurdity is in the midst of what is already absurd—then we have the play of fancy without the sense of ineptitude. Things amuse us in the mouth of a fool that would not amuse us in that of a gentleman; a fact which shows how little incongruity and degradation have to do with our pleasure in the comic. In fact, there is a kind of congruity and method even in fooling. The incongruous and the degraded displease us even there, as by their nature they must at all times. The shock which they bring may sometimes be the occasion of a subsequent pleasure, by attracting our attention, or by stimulating passions, such as scorn, or cruelty, or self-satisfaction (for there is a good deal of malice in our love of fun); but the incongruity and degradation, as such, always remain unpleasant. The pleasure comes from the inward rationality and movement of the fiction, not from its inconsistency with anything else. There are a great many topsy-turvy worlds possible to our fancy, into which we like to drop at times. We enjoy the stimulation and the shaking up of our wits. It is like getting into a new posture, or hearing a new song.

Nonsense is good only because common sense is so limited. For reason, after all, is one convention picked out of a thousand. We love expansion, not disorder, and when we attain freedom without incongruity we have a much greater and a much purer delight. The excellence of wit can dispense with absurdity. For on the same prosaic background of common sense, a novelty might have appeared that was not absurd, that stimulated the attention quite as much as the ridiculous, without so baffling the intelligence. This purer and more thoroughly delightful amusement comes from what we call wit.

§ 62. WIT. Wit also depends upon transformation and substitution of ideas. It has been said to consist in quick association by similarity. The substitution must here be valid, however, and the similarity real, though unforeseen. Unexpected justness makes wit, as sudden incongruity makes pleasant foolishness. It is characteristic of wit to penetrate into hidden depths of things, to pick out there some telling circumstance or relation, by noting which the whole object appears in a new and clearer light. Wit often seems malicious because analysis in discovering common traits and universal principles assimilates things at the poles of being; it can apply to cookery the formulas of theology, and find in the human heart a case of the fulcrum and lever. We commonly keep the departments of experience distinct; we think the different principles hold in each and that the dignity of spirit is inconsistent with the explanation of it by physical analogy, and the meanness of matter unworthy of being an illustration of moral truths. Love must not be classed under physical cravings, nor faith under hypnotization. When, therefore, an original mind overleaps these boundaries, and recasts its categories, mixing up our old classifications, we feel that the values of things are also confused. But these depended upon a deeper relation, upon their response to human needs and aspirations. All that can be changed by the exercise of intelligence is our sense of the unity and homogeneity of the world. We may come to hold an object of thought in less isolated respect, and another in less hasty derision; but the pleasures we derive from all, or our total happiness and wonder, will hardly be diminished. For this reason the malicious or destructive character of intelligence must not be regarded as fundamental. Wit belittles one thing and dignifies another; and its comparisons are as often flattering as ironical.

The same process of mind that we observed in wit gives rise to those effects we call charming, brilliant, or inspired. When Shakespeare says,

> Come and kiss me, *sweet and twenty,*
> Youth's a stuff will not endure,

the fancy of the phrase consists in a happy substitution, a merry way of saying something both true and tender. And where could we find a more exquisite charm? So, to take a weightier example, when St. Augustine says the virtues of the pagans were *splendid vices,* we have—at least if we catch the full meaning—a pungent assimilation of contrary things, by force of a powerful principle; a triumph of theory, the boldness of which can only be matched by its consistency. In fact, a phrase could not be more brilliant, or better condense one theology and two civilizations. The Latin mind is particularly capable of this sort of excellence. Tacitus alone could furnish a hundred examples. It goes with the power of satirical and bitter eloquence, a sort of scornful rudeness of intelligence, that makes for the core of a passion or of a character, and affixes to it a more or less scandalous label. For in our analytical zeal it is often possible to condense and abstract too much. Reality is more fluid and elusive than reason, and has, as it were, more dimensions than are known even to the latest geometry. Hence the understanding, when not suffused with some glow of sympathetic emotion or some touch of mysticism, gives but a dry, crude image of the world. The quality of wit inspires more admiration than confidence. It is a merit we should miss little in any one we love.

The same principle, however, can have more sentimental embodiments. When our substitutions are brought on by the excitement of generous emotion, we call wit inspiration. There is the same finding of new analogies, and likening of disparate things; there is the same transformation of our apperception. But the brilliancy is here not only penetrating, but also exalting. For instance:

Peace, peace, he is not dead, he doth not sleep,
  He hath awakened from the dream of life:
'Tis we that wrapped in stormy visions keep
  With phantoms an unprofitable strife.

There is here paradox, and paradox justified by reflection. The poet analyzes, and analyzes without reserve. The dream, the storm, the phantoms, and the unprofitableness could easily make a satirical picture. But the mood is transmuted; the mind takes an upward flight, with a sense of liberation from the convention it dissolves, and of freer motion in the vagueness beyond. The disintegration of our ideal here leads to mysticism, and because of this effort towards transcendence, the brilliancy becomes sublime.

§ 63. HUMOUR. A different mood can give a different direction to the same processes. The sympathy by which we reproduce the feeling of another, is always very much opposed to the æsthetic attitude to which the whole world is merely a stimulus to our sensibility. In the tragic, we have seen how the sympathetic feeling, by which suffering is appreciated and shared, has to be overlaid by many incidental æsthetic pleasures, if the resulting effect is to be on the whole good. We have also seen how the only way in which the ridiculous can be kept within the sphere of the æsthetically good is abstracting it from its relations, and treating it as an independent and curious stimulus; we should stop laughing and begin to be annoyed if we tried to make sense out of our absurdity. The less sympathy we have with men the more exquisite is our enjoyment of their folly: satirical delight is closely akin to cruelty. Defect and mishap stimulate our fancy, as blood and tortures excite in us the passions of the beast of prey. The more this inhuman attitude yields to sympathy and reason, the less are folly and error capable of amusing us. It would therefore seem impossible that we should be pleased by the foibles or absurdities of those we love. And in fact we never enjoy seeing our own persons in a satirical light, or any one else for whom we really feel affection. Even in farces, the hero and heroine are seldom made ridiculous, because that would jar upon the sympathy with which we are expected to regard them. Nevertheless, the essence of what we call humour is that amusing weaknesses should be combined with an amicable humanity. Whether it be in the way of ingenuity, or oddity, or drollery, the humorous person must have an absurd side, or be placed in an absurd situation. Yet this comic aspect, at which we ought to wince, seems to endear the character all the more. This is a parallel case to that of tragedy, where the depth of the woe we sympathize with seems to add to our satisfaction. And the explanation of the paradox is the same. We do not enjoy the expression of evil, but only the pleasant excitements that come with it; namely, the physical stimulus and the expression of good. In tragedy, the misfortunes help to give the impression of truth, and to bring out the noble qualities of the hero, but are in themselves depressing, so much so that over-sensitive people cannot enjoy the beauty of the representation. So also in humour, the painful suggestions are felt as such, and need to be overbalanced by agreeable elements. These come from both directions, from the æsthetic and the sympathetic reaction. On the one hand there is the sensuous and merely perceptive stimulation, the novelty, the movement, the vivacity of the spectacle. On the other hand, there is the luxury of imaginative sympathy, the mental assimilation of another congenial experience, the expansion into another life.

The juxtaposition of these two pleasures produces just that tension and complication in which the humorous consists. We are satirical, and we are friendly at the same time. The consciousness of the friendship gives a regretful and tender touch to the satire, and the sting of the satire makes the friendship a trifle humble and sad. Don Quixote is mad; he is old, useless, and ridiculous, but he is the soul of honour, and in all his laughable adventures we follow him like the ghost of our better selves. We enjoy his discomfitures too much to wish he had been a perfect Amadis; and we have besides a shrewd suspicion that he is the only kind of Amadis there can ever be in this world. At the same time it does us good to see the courage of his idealism, the ingenuity of his wit, and the simplicity of his goodness. But how shall we reconcile our sympathy with his dream and our perception of its absurdity? The situation is contradictory. We are drawn to some different point of view, from which the comedy may no longer seem so amusing. As humour becomes deep and really different from satire, it changes into pathos, and passes out of the sphere of the comic altogether. The mischances that were to amuse us as scoffers now grieve us as men, and the value of the representation depends on the touches of beauty and seriousness with which it is adorned.

§ 64. THE GROTESQUE. Something analogous to humour can appear in plastic forms, when we call it the grotesque. This is an interesting effect produced by such a transformation of an ideal type as exaggerates one of its elements or combines it with other types. The real excellence of this, like that of all fiction, consists in re-creation; in the formation of a thing which nature has not, but might conceivably have offered. We call these inventions comic and grotesque when we are considering their divergence from the natural rather than their inward possibility. But the latter constitutes their real charm; and the more we study and develope them, the better we understand it. The incongruity with the conventional type then disappears, and what was impossible and ridiculous at first takes its place among recognized ideals. The centaur and the satyr are no longer grotesque; the type is accepted. And the grotesqueness of an individual has essentially the same nature. If we like the inward harmony, the characteristic balance of his features, we are able to disengage this individual from the class into which we were trying to force him; we can forget the expectation which he was going to disappoint. The ugliness then disappears, and only the reassertion of the old habit and demand can make us regard him as in any way extravagant.

What appears as grotesque may be intrinsically inferior or superior to the normal. That is a question of its abstract material and form. But until the new object impresses its form on our imagination, so that we can grasp its unity and proportion, it appears to us as a jumble and distortion of other forms. If this confusion is absolute, the object is simply null; it does not exist æsthetically, except by virtue of materials. But if the confusion is not absolute, and we have an inkling of the unity and character in the midst of the strangeness of the form, then we have the grotesque. It is the half-formed, the perplexed, and the suggestively monstrous.

The analogy to the comic is very close, as we can readily conceive that it should be. In the comic we have this same juxtaposition of a new and an old idea, and if the new is not futile and really inconceivable, it may in time establish itself in the mind, and cease to be ludicrous. Good wit is novel truth, as the good grotesque is novel beauty. But there are natural conditions of organization, and we must not mistake every mutilation for the creation of a new form. The tendency of nature to establish well-marked species of animals shows what various combinations are most stable in the face of physical forces, and there is a fitness also for survival in the mind, which is determined by the relation of any form to our fixed method of perception. New things are therefore generally bad because, as has been well said, they are incapable of becoming old. A thousand originalities are produced by defect of faculty, for one that is produced by genius. For in the pursuit of beauty, as in that of truth, an infinite number of paths lead to failure, and only one to success.

§ 65. THE POSSIBILITY OF FINITE PERFECTION. If these observations have any accuracy, they confirm this important truth,— that no æsthetic value is really founded on the experience or the suggestion of evil. This conclusion will doubtless seem the more interesting if we think of its possible extension to the field of ethics and of the implied vindication of the ideals of moral perfection as something essentially definable and attainable. But without insisting on an analogy to ethics, which might be misleading, we may hasten to state the principle which emerges from our analysis of expression. Expressiveness may be found in any one thing that suggests another, or draws from association with that other any of its emotional colouring. There may, therefore, of course, be an expressiveness of evil; but this expressiveness will not have any æsthetic value. The description or suggestion of suffering may have a worth as science or discipline, but can never in itself enhance any beauty. Tragedy and comedy please in spite of this expressiveness and not by virtue of it; and except for the pleasures they give, they have no place among the fine arts. Nor have they, in such a case, any place in human life at all; unless they are instruments of some practical purpose and serve to preach a moral, or achieve a bad notoriety. For ugly things can attract attention, although they cannot keep it; and the scandal of a new horror may secure a certain vulgar admiration which follows whatever is momentarily conspicuous, and which is attained ever by crime. Such admiration, however, has nothing æsthetic about it, and is only made possible by the bluntness of our sense of beauty.

The effect of the pathetic and comic is therefore never pure; since the expression of some evil is mixed up with those elements by which the whole appeals to us. These elements we have seen to be the truth of the presentation, which involves the pleasures of recognition and comprehension, the beauty of the medium, and the concomitant expression of things intrinsically good. To these sources all the æsthetic value of comic and tragic is due; and the sympathetic emotion which arises from the spectacle of evil must never be allowed to overpower these pleasures of contemplation, else the entire object becomes distasteful and loses its excuse for being. Too exclusive a relish for the comic and pathetic is accordingly a sign of bad taste and of comparative insensibility to beauty.

This situation has generally been appreciated in the practice of the arts, where effect is perpetually studied; but the greatest care has not always succeeded in avoiding the dangers of the pathetic, and history is full of failures due to bombast, carica-ture, and unmitigated horror. In all these the effort to be ex-pressive has transgressed the conditions of pleasing effect. For the creative and imitative impulse is indiscriminate. It does not con-sider the eventual beauty of the effect, but only the blind in-stinct of self-expression. Hence an untrained and not naturally sensitive mind cannot distinguish or produce anything good. This critical incapacity has always been a cause of failure and a just ground for ridicule; but it remained for some thinkers of our time—a time of little art and much undisciplined production —to erect this abuse into a principle and declare that the essence of beauty is to express the artist and not to delight the world. But the conditions of effect, and the possibility of pleasing, are the only criterion of what is capable and worthy of expression. Art exists and has value by its adaptation to these universal conditions of beauty.

Nothing but the good of life enters into the texture of the beautiful. What charms us in the comic, what stirs us in the sub-lime and touches us in the pathetic, is a glimpse of some good; imperfection has value only as an incipient perfection. Could the labours and sufferings of life be reduced, and a better harmony between man and nature be established, nothing would be lost to the arts; for the pure and ultimate value of the comic is discovery, of the pathetic, love, of the sublime, exaltation; and these would still subsist. Indeed, they would all be increased; and it has ever been, accordingly, in the happiest and most prosperous moments of humanity, when the mind and the world were knit into a brief embrace, that natural beauty has been best perceived, and art has won its triumphs. But it sometimes happens, in moments less propitious, that the soul is subdued to what it works in, and loses its power of idealization and hope. By a pathetic and superstitious self-depreciation, we then punish ourselves for the imperfection of nature. Awed by the magnitude of a reality that we can no longer conceive as free from evil, we try to assert that its evil also is a good; and we poison the very essence of the good to make its extension uni-versal. We confuse the causal connexion of those things in na-ture which we call good or evil by an adventitious denomination, with the logical opposition between good and evil themselves; because one generation makes room for another, we say death is necessary to life; and because the causes of sorrow and joy are so mingled in this world, we cannot conceive how, in a better world, they might be disentangled.

This incapacity of the imagination to reconstruct the conditions of life and build the frame of things nearer to the heart's desire is very fatal to a steady loyalty to what is noble and fine. We surrender ourselves to a kind of miscellaneous appreciation, without standard or goal; and calling every vexatious apparition by the name of beauty, we become incapable of discriminating its excellence or feeling its value. We need to clarify our ideals, and enliven our vision of perfection. No atheism is so terrible as the absence of an ultimate ideal, nor could any failure of power be more contrary to human nature than the failure of moral imagination, or more incompatible with healthy life. For we have faculties, and habits, and impulses. These are the basis of our demands. And these demands, although variable, constitute an ever-present intrinsic standard of value by which we feel and judge. The ideal is immanent in them; for the ideal means that environment in which our faculties would find their freest employment, and their most congenial world. Perfection would be nothing but life under those conditions. Accordingly our consciousness of the ideal becomes distinct in proportion as we advance in virtue and in proportion to the vigour and definiteness with which our faculties work. When the vital harmony is complete, when the *act* is *pure*, faith in perfection passes into vision. That man is unhappy indeed, who in all his life has had no glimpse of perfection, who in the ecstasy of love, or in the delight of contemplation, has never been able to say: It is attained. Such moments of inspiration are the source of the arts, which have no higher function than to renew them.

A work of art is indeed a monument to such a moment, the memorial to such a vision; and its charm varies with its power of recalling us from the distractions of common life to the joy of a more natural and perfect activity.

§ 66. THE STABILITY OF THE IDEAL. The perfection thus revealed is relative to our nature and faculties; if it were not, it could have no value for us. It is revealed to us in brief moments, but it is not for that reason an unstable or fantastic thing. Human attention inevitably flickers; we survey things in succession, and our acts of synthesis and our realization of fact are only occasional.

This is the tenure of all our possessions; we are not uninter-
ruptedly conscious of ourselves, our physical environment, our
ruling passions, or our deepest conviction. What wonder, then,
that we are not constantly conscious of that perfection which
is the implicit ideal of all our preferences and desires? We view
it only in parts, as passion or perception successively directs our
attention to its various elements. Some of us never try to conceive it in its totality. Yet our whole life is an act of worship
to this unknown divinity; every heartfelt prayer is offered before
one or another of its images.

This ideal of perfection varies, indeed, but only with the variations of our nature of which it is the counterpart and entelechy.
There is perhaps no more frivolous notion than that to which
Schopenhauer has given a new currency, that a good, once attained, loses all its value. The instability of our attention, the
need of rest and repair in our organs, makes a round of objects
necessary to our minds; but we turn from a beautiful thing, as
from a truth or a friend, only to return incessantly, and with
increasing appreciation. Nor do we lose all the benefit of our
achievements in the intervals between our vivid realizations of
what we have gained. The tone of the mind is permanently
raised; and we live with that general sense of steadfastness and
resource, which is perhaps the kernel of happiness. Knowledge,
affection, religion, and beauty are not less constant influences
in a man's life because his consciousness of them is intermittent.
Even when absent, they fill the chambers of the mind with a
kind of fragrance. They have a continual efficacy, as well as a
perennial worth.

There are, indeed, other objects of desire that if attained
leave nothing but restlessness and dissatisfaction behind them.
These are the objects pursued by fools. That such objects ever
attract us is a proof of the disorganization of our nature,
which drives us in contrary directions and is at war with itself.
If we had attained anything like steadiness of thought or fixity
of character, if we knew ourselves, we should know also our
inalienable satisfactions. To say that all goods become worthless
in possession is either a piece of superficial satire that intentionally denies the normal in order to make the abnormal seem more
shocking, or else it is a confession of frivolity, a confession that,
as an idiot never learns to distinguish reality amid the phantasms
of his brain, so we have never learned to distinguish true goods
amid our extravagances of whim and passion. That true
goods exist is nevertheless a fact of moral experience. "A thing of

beauty is a joy for ever"; a great affection, a clear thought, a profound and well-tried faith, are eternal possessions. And this is not merely a fact, to be asserted upon the authority of those who know it by experience. It is a psychological necessity. While we retain the same senses, we must get the same impressions from the same objects; while we keep our instincts and passions, we must pursue the same goods; while we have the same powers of imagination, we must experience the same delight in their exercise. Age brings about, of course, variation in all these particulars, and the susceptibility of two individuals is never exactly similar. But the eventual decay of our personal energies does not destroy the natural value of objects, so long as the same will embodies itself in other minds, and human nature subsists in the world. The sun is not now unreal because each one of us in succession, and all of us in the end, must close our eyes upon it; and yet the sun exists for us only because we perceive it. The ideal has the same conditions of being, but has this advantage over the sun, that we cannot know if its light is ever destined to fail us.

There is then a broad foundation of identity in our nature, by virtue of which we live in a common world, and have an art and a religion in common. That the ideal should be constant within these limits is as inevitable as that it should vary beyond them. And so long as we exist and recognize ourselves individually as persons or collectively as human, we must recognize also our immanent ideal, the realization of which would constitute perfection for us. That ideal cannot be destroyed except in proportion as we ourselves perish. An absolute perfection, independent of human nature and its variations, may interest the metaphysician; but the artist and the man will be satisfied with a perfection that is inseparable from the consciousness of mankind, since it is at once the natural vision of the imagination, and the rational goal of the will.

§ 67. Conclusion. We have now studied the sense of beauty in what seem to be its fundamental manifestations, and in some of the more striking complications which it undergoes. In surveying so broad a field we stand in need of some classification and subdivision; and we have chosen the familiar one of matter, form, and expression, as least likely to lead us into needless artificiality. But artificiality there must always be in the discursive description of anything given in consciousness. Psychology attempts what is perhaps impossible, namely, the anatomy of life. Mind is a fluid; the lights and shadows that flicker through it have no real boundaries, and no possibility of permanence. Our whole classification of mental facts is borrowed from the physical conditions or expressions of them. The very senses are distinguished because of the readiness with which we can isolate their outer organs. Ideas can be identified only by identifying their objects. Feelings are recognized by their outer expression, and when we try to recall an emotion, we must do so by recalling the circumstances in which it occurred.

In distinguishing, then, in our sense of beauty, an appreciation of sensible material, one of abstract form, and another of associated values, we have been merely following the established method of psychology, the only one by which it is possible to analyze the mind. We have distinguished the elements of the object, and treated the feeling as if it were composed of corresponding parts. The worlds of nature and fancy, which are the object of æsthetic feeling, can be divided into parts in space and time. We can then distinguish the material of things from the various forms it may successively assume; we can distinguish, also, the earlier and the later impressions made by the same object; and we can ascertain the coexistence of one impression with another, or with the memory of others. But æsthetic feeling itself has no parts, and this physiology of its causes is not a description of its proper nature.

Beauty as we feel it is something indescribable: what it is or what it means can never be said. By appealing to experiment and memory we can show that this feeling varies as certain things vary in the objective conditions; that it varies with the frequency, for instance, with which a form has been presented, or with the associates which that form has had in the past. This will justify a description of the feeling as composed of the various contributions of these objects. But the feeling itself knows nothing of composition nor contributions. It is an affection of the soul, a consciousness of joy and security, a pang, a dream, a pure pleasure. It suffuses an object without telling why; nor has it any need to ask the question. It justifies itself and the vision it gilds; nor is there any meaning in seeking for a cause of it, in this inward sense. Beauty exists for the same reason that the object which is beautiful exists, or the world in which that object lies, or we that look upon both. It is an experience: there is nothing more to say about it. Indeed, if we look at things teleologically, and as they ultimately justify themselves to the heart, beauty is of all things what least calls for explanation. For matter and space and time and principles of reason and of evolution, all are ultimately brute, unaccountable data. We may describe what actually is, but it might have been otherwise, and the mystery of its being is as baffling and dark as ever.

But we,—the minds that ask all questions and judge of the validity of all answers,—we are not ourselves independent of this world in which we live. We sprang from it, and our relations in it determine all our instincts and satisfactions. This final questioning and sense of mystery is an unsatisfied craving which nature has her way of stilling. Now we only ask for reasons when we are surprised. If we had no expectations we should have no surprises. And what gives us expectation is the spontaneous direction of our thought, determined by the structure of our brain and the effects of our experience. If our spontaneous thoughts came to run in harmony with the course of nature, if our expectations were then continually fulfilled, the sense of mystery would vanish. We should be incapable of asking why the world existed or had such a nature, just as we are now little inclined to ask why anything is right, but mightily disinclined to give up asking why anything is wrong.

This satisfaction of our reason, due to the harmony between our nature and our experience, is partially realized already. The sense of beauty is its realization. When our senses and imagination find what they crave, when the world so shapes itself or so moulds the mind that the correspondence between them is perfect, then perception is pleasure, and existence needs no apology. The duality which is the condition of conflict disappears. There is no inward standard different from the outward fact with which that outward fact may be compared. A unification of this kind is the goal of our intelligence and of our affection, quite as much as of our æsthetic sense; but we have in those departments fewer examples of success. In the heat of speculation or of love there may come moments of equal perfection, but they are very unstable. The reason and the heart remain deeply unsatisfied. But the eye finds in nature, and in some supreme achievements of art, constant and fuller satisfaction. For the eye is quick, and seems to have been more docile to the education of life than the heart or the reason of man, and able sooner to adapt itself to the reality. Beauty therefore seems to be the clearest manifestation of perfection, and the best evidence of its possibility. If perfection is, as it should be, the ultimate justification of being, we may understand the ground of the moral dignity of beauty. Beauty is a pledge of the possible conformity between the soul and nature, and consequently a ground of faith in the supremacy of the good.

INDEX

A CATALOG OF SELECTED

DOVER BOOKS

IN ALL FIELDS OF INTEREST

A CATALOG OF SELECTED DOVER
BOOKS IN ALL FIELDS OF INTEREST

DRAWINGS OF REMBRANDT, edited by Seymour Slive. Updated Lippmann, Hofstede de Groot edition, with definitive scholarly apparatus. All portraits, biblical sketches, landscapes, nudes. Oriental figures, classical studies, together with selection of work by followers. 550 illustrations. Total of 630pp. 9⅜ × 12¼.
21485-0, 21486-9 Pa., Two-vol. set $25.00

GHOST AND HORROR STORIES OF AMBROSE BIERCE, Ambrose Bierce. 24 tales vividly imagined, strangely prophetic, and decades ahead of their time in technical skill: "The Damned Thing," "An Inhabitant of Carcosa," "The Eyes of the Panther," "Moxon's Master," and 20 more. 199pp. 5⅜ × 8½. 20767-6 Pa. $3.95

ETHICAL WRITINGS OF MAIMONIDES, Maimonides. Most significant ethical works of great medieval sage, newly translated for utmost precision, readability. Laws Concerning Character Traits, Eight Chapters, more. 192pp. 5⅜ × 8½.
24522-5 Pa. $4.50

THE EXPLORATION OF THE COLORADO RIVER AND ITS CANYONS, J. W. Powell. Full text of Powell's 1,000-mile expedition down the fabled Colorado in 1869. Superb account of terrain, geology, vegetation, Indians, famine, mutiny, treacherous rapids, mighty canyons, during exploration of last unknown part of continental U.S. 400pp. 5⅜ × 8½. 20094-9 Pa. $6.95

HISTORY OF PHILOSOPHY, Julián Marías. Clearest one-volume history on the market. Every major philosopher and dozens of others, to Existentialism and later. 505pp. 5⅜ × 8½. 21739-6 Pa. $8.50

ALL ABOUT LIGHTNING, Martin A. Uman. Highly readable non-technical survey of nature and causes of lightning, thunderstorms, ball lightning, St. Elmo's Fire, much more. Illustrated. 192pp. 5⅜ × 8½. 25237-X Pa. $5.95

SAILING ALONE AROUND THE WORLD, Captain Joshua Slocum. First man to sail around the world, alone, in small boat. One of great feats of seamanship told in delightful manner. 67 illustrations. 294pp. 5⅜ × 8½. 20326-3 Pa. $4.95

LETTERS AND NOTES ON THE MANNERS, CUSTOMS AND CONDITIONS OF THE NORTH AMERICAN INDIANS, George Catlin. Classic account of life among Plains Indians: ceremonies, hunt, warfare, etc. 312 plates. 572pp. of text. 6⅛ × 9¼. 22118-0, 22119-9 Pa. Two-vol. set $15.90

ALASKA: The Harriman Expedition, 1899, John Burroughs, John Muir, et al. Informative, engrossing accounts of two-month, 9,000-mile expedition. Native peoples, wildlife, forests, geography, salmon industry, glaciers, more. Profusely illustrated. 240 black-and-white line drawings. 124 black-and-white photographs. 3 maps. Index. 576pp. 5⅜ × 8½. 25109-8 Pa. $11.95

SUNDIALS, Albert Waugh. Far and away the best, most thorough coverage of ideas, mathematics concerned, types, construction, adjusting anywhere. Over 100 illustrations. 230pp. 5⅜ × 8½. 22947-5 Pa. $4.50

PICTURE HISTORY OF THE NORMANDIE: With 190 Illustrations, Frank O. Braynard. Full story of legendary French ocean liner: Art Deco interiors, design innovations, furnishings, celebrities, maiden voyage, tragic fire, much more. Extensive text. 144pp. 8⅜ × 11¾. 25257-4 Pa. $9.95

THE FIRST AMERICAN COOKBOOK: A Facsimile of "American Cookery," 1796, Amelia Simmons. Facsimile of the first American-written cookbook published in the United States contains authentic recipes for colonial favorites—pumpkin pudding, winter squash pudding, spruce beer, Indian slapjacks, and more. Introductory Essay and Glossary of colonial cooking terms. 80pp. 5⅜ × 8½. 24710-4 Pa. $3.50

101 PUZZLES IN THOUGHT AND LOGIC, C. R. Wylie, Jr. Solve murders and robberies, find out which fishermen are liars, how a blind man could possibly identify a color—purely by your own reasoning! 107pp. 5⅜ × 8½. 20367-0 Pa. $2.50

THE BOOK OF WORLD-FAMOUS MUSIC—CLASSICAL, POPULAR AND FOLK, James J. Fuld. Revised and enlarged republication of landmark work in musico-bibliography. Full information about nearly 1,000 songs and compositions including first lines of music and lyrics. New supplement. Index. 800pp. 5⅜ × 8¼. 24857-7 Pa. $14.95

ANTHROPOLOGY AND MODERN LIFE, Franz Boas. Great anthropologist's classic treatise on race and culture. Introduction by Ruth Bunzel. Only inexpensive paperback edition. 255pp. 5⅜ × 8½. 25245-0 Pa. $5.95

THE TALE OF PETER RABBIT, Beatrix Potter. The inimitable Peter's terrifying adventure in Mr. McGregor's garden, with all 27 wonderful, full-color Potter illustrations. 55pp. 4¼ × 5½. (Available in U.S. only) 22827-4 Pa. $1.75

THREE PROPHETIC SCIENCE FICTION NOVELS, H. G. Wells. *When the Sleeper Wakes, A Story of the Days to Come* and *The Time Machine* (full version). 335pp. 5⅜ × 8½. (Available in U.S. only) 20605-X Pa. $5.95

APICIUS COOKERY AND DINING IN IMPERIAL ROME, edited and translated by Joseph Dommers Vehling. Oldest known cookbook in existence offers readers a clear picture of what foods Romans ate, how they prepared them, etc. 49 illustrations. 301pp. 6⅛ × 9¼. 23563-7 Pa. $6.50

SHAKESPEARE LEXICON AND QUOTATION DICTIONARY, Alexander Schmidt. Full definitions, locations, shades of meaning of every word in plays and poems. More than 50,000 exact quotations. 1,485pp. 6½ × 9¼. 22726-X, 22727-8 Pa., Two-vol. set $27.90

THE WORLD'S GREAT SPEECHES, edited by Lewis Copeland and Lawrence W. Lamm. Vast collection of 278 speeches from Greeks to 1970. Powerful and effective models; unique look at history. 842pp. 5⅜ × 8½. 20468-5 Pa. $11.95

THE BLUE FAIRY BOOK, Andrew Lang. The first, most famous collection, with many familiar tales: Little Red Riding Hood, Aladdin and the Wonderful Lamp, Puss in Boots, Sleeping Beauty, Hansel and Gretel, Rumpelstiltskin; 37 in all. 138 illustrations. 390pp. 5⅜ × 8½. 21437-0 Pa. $5.95

THE STORY OF THE CHAMPIONS OF THE ROUND TABLE, Howard Pyle. Sir Launcelot, Sir Tristram and Sir Percival in spirited adventures of love and triumph retold in Pyle's inimitable style. 50 drawings, 31 full-page. xviii + 329pp. 6½ × 9¼. 21883-X Pa. $6.95

AUDUBON AND HIS JOURNALS, Maria Audubon. Unmatched two-volume portrait of the great artist, naturalist and author contains his journals, an excellent biography by his granddaughter, expert annotations by the noted ornithologist, Dr. Elliott Coues, and 37 superb illustrations. Total of 1,200pp. 5⅜ × 8.
Vol. I 25143-8 Pa. $8.95
Vol. II 25144-6 Pa. $8.95

GREAT DINOSAUR HUNTERS AND THEIR DISCOVERIES, Edwin H. Colbert. Fascinating, lavishly illustrated chronicle of dinosaur research, 1820's to 1960. Achievements of Cope, Marsh, Brown, Buckland, Mantell, Huxley, many others. 384pp. 5¼ × 8¼. 24701-5 Pa. $6.95

THE TASTEMAKERS, Russell Lynes. Informal, illustrated social history of American taste 1850's–1950's. First popularized categories Highbrow, Lowbrow, Middlebrow. 129 illustrations. New (1979) afterword. 384pp. 6 × 9.
23993-4 Pa. $6.95

DOUBLE CROSS PURPOSES, Ronald A. Knox. A treasure hunt in the Scottish Highlands, an old map, unidentified corpse, surprise discoveries keep reader guessing in this cleverly intricate tale of financial skullduggery. 2 black-and-white maps. 320pp. 5⅜ × 8½. (Available in U.S. only) 25032-6 Pa. $5.95

AUTHENTIC VICTORIAN DECORATION AND ORNAMENTATION IN FULL COLOR: 46 Plates from "Studies in Design," Christopher Dresser. Superb full-color lithographs reproduced from rare original portfolio of a major Victorian designer. 48pp. 9¼ × 12¼. 25083-0 Pa. $7.95

PRIMITIVE ART, Franz Boas. Remains the best text ever prepared on subject, thoroughly discussing Indian, African, Asian, Australian, and, especially, Northern American primitive art. Over 950 illustrations show ceramics, masks, totem poles, weapons, textiles, paintings, much more. 376pp. 5⅜ × 8. 20025-6 Pa. $6.95

SIDELIGHTS ON RELATIVITY, Albert Einstein. Unabridged republication of two lectures delivered by the great physicist in 1920–21. *Ether and Relativity* and *Geometry and Experience*. Elegant ideas in non-mathematical form, accessible to intelligent layman. vi + 56pp. 5⅜ × 8½. 24511-X Pa. $2.95

THE WIT AND HUMOR OF OSCAR WILDE, edited by Alvin Redman. More than 1,000 ripostes, paradoxes, wisecracks: Work is the curse of the drinking classes, I can resist everything except temptation, etc. 258pp. 5⅜ × 8½. 20602-5 Pa. $4.50

ADVENTURES WITH A MICROSCOPE, Richard Headstrom. 59 adventures with clothing fibers, protozoa, ferns and lichens, roots and leaves, much more. 142 illustrations. 232pp. 5⅜ × 8½. 23471-1 Pa. $3.95

PLANTS OF THE BIBLE, Harold N. Moldenke and Alma L. Moldenke. Standard reference to all 230 plants mentioned in Scriptures. Latin name, biblical reference, uses, modern identity, much more. Unsurpassed encyclopedic resource for scholars, botanists, nature lovers, students of Bible. Bibliography. Indexes. 123 black-and-white illustrations. 384pp. 6 × 9.   25069-5 Pa. $8.95

FAMOUS AMERICAN WOMEN: A Biographical Dictionary from Colonial Times to the Present, Robert McHenry, ed. From Pocahontas to Rosa Parks, 1,035 distinguished American women documented in separate biographical entries. Accurate, up-to-date data, numerous categories, spans 400 years. Indices. 493pp. 6½ × 9¼.   24523-3 Pa. $9.95

THE FABULOUS INTERIORS OF THE GREAT OCEAN LINERS IN HISTORIC PHOTOGRAPHS, William H. Miller, Jr. Some 200 superb photographs capture exquisite interiors of world's great "floating palaces"—1890's to 1980's: *Titanic, Ile de France, Queen Elizabeth, United States, Europa*, more. Approx. 200 black-and-white photographs. Captions. Text. Introduction. 160pp. 8⅜ × 11¼.
24756-2 Pa. $9.95

THE GREAT LUXURY LINERS, 1927–1954: A Photographic Record, William H. Miller, Jr. Nostalgic tribute to heyday of ocean liners. 186 photos of Ile de France, Normandie, Leviathan, Queen Elizabeth, United States, many others. Interior and exterior views. Introduction. Captions. 160pp. 9 × 12.
24056-8 Pa. $9.95

A NATURAL HISTORY OF THE DUCKS, John Charles Phillips. Great landmark of ornithology offers complete detailed coverage of nearly 200 species and subspecies of ducks: gadwall, sheldrake, merganser, pintail, many more. 74 full-color plates, 102 black-and-white. Bibliography. Total of 1,920pp. 8⅜ × 11¼.
25141-1, 25142-X Cloth. Two-vol. set $100.00

THE SEAWEED HANDBOOK: An Illustrated Guide to Seaweeds from North Carolina to Canada, Thomas F. Lee. Concise reference covers 78 species. Scientific and common names, habitat, distribution, more. Finding keys for easy identification. 224pp. 5⅜ × 8½.   25215-9 Pa. $5.95

THE TEN BOOKS OF ARCHITECTURE: The 1755 Leoni Edition, Leon Battista Alberti. Rare classic helped introduce the glories of ancient architecture to the Renaissance. 68 black-and-white plates. 336pp. 8⅜ × 11¼.   25239-6 Pa. $14.95

MISS MACKENZIE, Anthony Trollope. Minor masterpieces by Victorian master unmasks many truths about life in 19th-century England. First inexpensive edition in years. 392pp. 5⅜ × 8½.   25201-9 Pa. $7.95

THE RIME OF THE ANCIENT MARINER, Gustave Doré, Samuel Taylor Coleridge. Dramatic engravings considered by many to be his greatest work. The terrifying space of the open sea, the storms and whirlpools of an unknown ocean, the ice of Antarctica, more—all rendered in a powerful, chilling manner. Full text. 38 plates. 77pp. 9¼ × 12.   22305-1 Pa. $4.95

THE EXPEDITIONS OF ZEBULON MONTGOMERY PIKE, Zebulon Montgomery Pike. Fascinating first-hand accounts (1805–6) of exploration of Mississippi River, Indian wars, capture by Spanish dragoons, much more. 1,088pp. 5⅜ × 8½.   25254-X, 25255-8 Pa. Two-vol. set $23.90

A CONCISE HISTORY OF PHOTOGRAPHY: Third Revised Edition, Helmut Gernsheim. Best one-volume history—camera obscura, photochemistry, daguerreotypes, evolution of cameras, film, more. Also artistic aspects—landscape, portraits, fine art, etc. 281 black-and-white photographs. 26 in color. 176pp. 8⅜ × 11¼. 25128-4 Pa. $12.95

THE DORÉ BIBLE ILLUSTRATIONS, Gustave Doré. 241 detailed plates from the Bible: the Creation scenes, Adam and Eve, Flood, Babylon, battle sequences, life of Jesus, etc. Each plate is accompanied by the verses from the King James version of the Bible. 241pp. 9 × 12. 23004-X Pa. $8.95

HUGGER-MUGGER IN THE LOUVRE, Elliot Paul. Second Homer Evans mystery-comedy. Theft at the Louvre involves sleuth in hilarious, madcap caper. "A knockout."—Books. 336pp. 5⅜ × 8½. 25185-3 Pa. $5.95

FLATLAND, E. A. Abbott. Intriguing and enormously popular science-fiction classic explores the complexities of trying to survive as a two-dimensional being in a three-dimensional world. Amusingly illustrated by the author. 16 illustrations. 103pp. 5⅜ × 8½. 20001-9 Pa. $2.25

THE HISTORY OF THE LEWIS AND CLARK EXPEDITION, Meriwether Lewis and William Clark, edited by Elliott Coues. Classic edition of Lewis and Clark's day-by-day journals that later became the basis for U.S. claims to Oregon and the West. Accurate and invaluable geographical, botanical, biological, meteorological and anthropological material. Total of 1,508pp. 5⅜ × 8½.
21268-8, 21269-6, 21270-X Pa. Three-vol. set $25.50

LANGUAGE, TRUTH AND LOGIC, Alfred J. Ayer. Famous, clear introduction to Vienna, Cambridge schools of Logical Positivism. Role of philosophy, elimination of metaphysics, nature of analysis, etc. 160pp. 5⅜ × 8½. (Available in U.S. and Canada only) 20010-8 Pa. $2.95

MATHEMATICS FOR THE NONMATHEMATICIAN, Morris Kline. Detailed, college-level treatment of mathematics in cultural and historical context, with numerous exercises. For liberal arts students. Preface. Recommended Reading Lists. Tables. Index. Numerous black-and-white figures. xvi + 641pp. 5⅜ × 8½.
24823-2 Pa. $11.95

28 SCIENCE FICTION STORIES, H. G. Wells. Novels, *Star Begotten* and *Men Like Gods,* plus 26 short stories: "Empire of the Ants," "A Story of the Stone Age," "The Stolen Bacillus," "In the Abyss," etc. 915pp. 5⅜ × 8½. (Available in U.S. only)
20265-8 Cloth. $10.95

HANDBOOK OF PICTORIAL SYMBOLS, Rudolph Modley. 3,250 signs and symbols, many systems in full; official or heavy commercial use. Arranged by subject. Most in Pictorial Archive series. 143pp. 8⅛ × 11. 23357-X Pa. $5.95

INCIDENTS OF TRAVEL IN YUCATAN, John L. Stephens. Classic (1843) exploration of jungles of Yucatan, looking for evidences of Maya civilization. Travel adventures, Mexican and Indian culture, etc. Total of 669pp. 5⅜ × 8½.
20926-1, 20927-X Pa., Two-vol. set $9.90

DEGAS: An Intimate Portrait, Ambroise Vollard. Charming, anecdotal memoir by famous art dealer of one of the greatest 19th-century French painters. 14 black-and-white illustrations. Introduction by Harold L. Van Doren. 96pp. 5⅜ × 8½.
25131-4 Pa. $3.95

PERSONAL NARRATIVE OF A PILGRIMAGE TO ALMANDINAH AND MECCAH, Richard Burton. Great travel classic by remarkably colorful personality. Burton, disguised as a Moroccan, visited sacred shrines of Islam, narrowly escaping death. 47 illustrations. 959pp. 5⅜ × 8½.   21217-3, 21218-1 Pa., Two-vol. set $17.90

PHRASE AND WORD ORIGINS, A. H. Holt. Entertaining, reliable, modern study of more than 1,200 colorful words, phrases, origins and histories. Much unexpected information. 254pp. 5⅜ × 8½.   20758-7 Pa. $5.95

THE RED THUMB MARK, R. Austin Freeman. In this first Dr. Thorndyke case, the great scientific detective draws fascinating conclusions from the nature of a single fingerprint. Exciting story, authentic science. 320pp. 5⅜ × 8½. (Available in U.S. only)   25210-8 Pa. $5.95

AN EGYPTIAN HIEROGLYPHIC DICTIONARY, E. A. Wallis Budge. Monumental work containing about 25,000 words or terms that occur in texts ranging from 3000 B.C. to 600 A.D. Each entry consists of a transliteration of the word, the word in hieroglyphs, and the meaning in English. 1,314pp. 6⅜ × 10.
23615-3, 23616-1 Pa., Two-vol. set $27.90

THE COMPLEAT STRATEGYST: Being a Primer on the Theory of Games of Strategy, J. D. Williams. Highly entertaining classic describes, with many illustrated examples, how to select best strategies in conflict situations. Prefaces. Appendices. xvi + 268pp. 5⅜ × 8½.   25101-2 Pa. $5.95

THE ROAD TO OZ, L. Frank Baum. Dorothy meets the Shaggy Man, little Button-Bright and the Rainbow's beautiful daughter in this delightful trip to the magical Land of Oz. 272pp. 5⅜ × 8.   25208-6 Pa. $4.95

POINT AND LINE TO PLANE, Wassily Kandinsky. Seminal exposition of role of point, line, other elements in non-objective painting. Essential to understanding 20th-century art. 127 illustrations. 192pp. 6½ × 9¼.   23808-3 Pa. $4.50

LADY ANNA, Anthony Trollope. Moving chronicle of Countess Lovel's bitter struggle to win for herself and daughter Anna their rightful rank and fortune— perhaps at cost of sanity itself. 384pp. 5⅜ × 8½.   24669-8 Pa. $6.95

EGYPTIAN MAGIC, E. A. Wallis Budge. Sums up all that is known about magic in Ancient Egypt: the role of magic in controlling the gods, powerful amulets that warded off evil spirits, scarabs of immortality, use of wax images, formulas and spells, the secret name, much more. 253pp. 5⅜ × 8½.   22681-6 Pa. $4.50

THE DANCE OF SIVA, Ananda Coomaraswamy. Preeminent authority unfolds the vast metaphysic of India: the revelation of her art, conception of the universe, social organization, etc. 27 reproductions of art masterpieces. 192pp. 5⅜ × 8½.
24817-8 Pa. $5.95

CHRISTMAS CUSTOMS AND TRADITIONS, Clement A. Miles. Origin, evolution, significance of religious, secular practices. Caroling, gifts, yule logs, much more. Full, scholarly yet fascinating; non-sectarian. 400pp. 5⅜ × 8½.
23354-5 Pa. $6.50

THE HUMAN FIGURE IN MOTION, Eadweard Muybridge. More than 4,500 stopped-action photos, in action series, showing undraped men, women, children jumping, lying down, throwing, sitting, wrestling, carrying, etc. 390pp. 7⅞ × 10⅝.
20204-6 Cloth. $19.95

THE MAN WHO WAS THURSDAY, Gilbert Keith Chesterton. Witty, fast-paced novel about a club of anarchists in turn-of-the-century London. Brilliant social, religious, philosophical speculations. 128pp. 5⅜ × 8½. 25121-7 Pa. $3.95

A CEZANNE SKETCHBOOK: Figures, Portraits, Landscapes and Still Lifes, Paul Cezanne. Great artist experiments with tonal effects, light, mass, other qualities in over 100 drawings. A revealing view of developing master painter, precursor of Cubism. 102 black-and-white illustrations. 144pp. 8¾ × 6⅜. 24790-2 Pa. $5.95

AN ENCYCLOPEDIA OF BATTLES: Accounts of Over 1,560 Battles from 1479 B.C. to the Present, David Eggenberger. Presents essential details of every major battle in recorded history, from the first battle of Megiddo in 1479 B.C. to Grenada in 1984. List of Battle Maps. New Appendix covering the years 1967–1984. Index. 99 illustrations. 544pp. 6½ × 9¼. 24913-1 Pa. $14.95

AN ETYMOLOGICAL DICTIONARY OF MODERN ENGLISH, Ernest Weekley. Richest, fullest work, by foremost British lexicographer. Detailed word histories. Inexhaustible. Total of 856pp. 6½ × 9¼.
21873-2, 21874-0 Pa., Two-vol. set $17.00

WEBSTER'S AMERICAN MILITARY BIOGRAPHIES, edited by Robert McHenry. Over 1,000 figures who shaped 3 centuries of American military history. Detailed biographies of Nathan Hale, Douglas MacArthur, Mary Hallaren, others. Chronologies of engagements, more. Introduction. Addenda. 1,033 entries in alphabetical order. xi + 548pp. 6½ × 9¼. (Available in U.S. only)
24758-9 Pa. $11.95

LIFE IN ANCIENT EGYPT, Adolf Erman. Detailed older account, with much not in more recent books: domestic life, religion, magic, medicine, commerce, and whatever else needed for complete picture. Many illustrations. 597pp. 5⅜ × 8½.
22632-8 Pa. $8.95

HISTORIC COSTUME IN PICTURES, Braun & Schneider. Over 1,450 costumed figures shown, covering a wide variety of peoples: kings, emperors, nobles, priests, servants, soldiers, scholars, townsfolk, peasants, merchants, courtiers, cavaliers, and more. 256pp. 8⅜ × 11¼. 23150-X Pa. $7.95

THE NOTEBOOKS OF LEONARDO DA VINCI, edited by J. P. Richter. Extracts from manuscripts reveal great genius; on painting, sculpture, anatomy, sciences, geography, etc. Both Italian and English. 186 ms. pages reproduced, plus 500 additional drawings, including studies for *Last Supper*, *Sforza* monument, etc. 860pp. 7⅞ × 10¾. (Available in U.S. only) 22572-0, 22573-9 Pa., Two-vol. set $25.90

THE ART NOUVEAU STYLE BOOK OF ALPHONSE MUCHA: All 72 Plates from "Documents Decoratifs" in Original Color, Alphonse Mucha. Rare copyright-free design portfolio by high priest of Art Nouveau. Jewelry, wallpaper, stained glass, furniture, figure studies, plant and animal motifs, etc. Only complete one-volume edition. 80pp. 9⅜ × 12¼. 24044-4 Pa. $8.95

ANIMALS: 1,419 COPYRIGHT-FREE ILLUSTRATIONS OF MAMMALS, BIRDS, FISH, INSECTS, ETC., edited by Jim Harter. Clear wood engravings present, in extremely lifelike poses, over 1,000 species of animals. One of the most extensive pictorial sourcebooks of its kind. Captions. Index. 284pp. 9 × 12. 23766-4 Pa. $9.95

OBELISTS FLY HIGH, C. Daly King. Masterpiece of American detective fiction, long out of print, involves murder on a 1935 transcontinental flight—"a very thrilling story"—NY Times. Unabridged and unaltered republication of the edition published by William Collins Sons & Co. Ltd., London, 1935. 288pp. 5⅜ × 8½. (Available in U.S. only) 25036-9 Pa. $4.95

VICTORIAN AND EDWARDIAN FASHION: A Photographic Survey, Alison Gernsheim. First fashion history completely illustrated by contemporary photographs. Full text plus 235 photos, 1840–1914, in which many celebrities appear. 240pp. 6½ × 9¼. 24205-6 Pa. $6.00

THE ART OF THE FRENCH ILLUSTRATED BOOK, 1700–1914, Gordon N. Ray. Over 630 superb book illustrations by Fragonard, Delacroix, Daumier, Doré, Grandville, Manet, Mucha, Steinlen, Toulouse-Lautrec and many others. Preface. Introduction. 633 halftones. Indices of artists, authors & titles, binders and provenances. Appendices. Bibliography. 608pp. 8⅜ × 11¼. 25086-5 Pa. $24.95

THE WONDERFUL WIZARD OF OZ, L. Frank Baum. Facsimile in full color of America's finest children's classic. 143 illustrations by W. W. Denslow. 267pp. 5⅜ × 8½. 20691-2 Pa. $5.95

FRONTIERS OF MODERN PHYSICS: New Perspectives on Cosmology, Relativity, Black Holes and Extraterrestrial Intelligence, Tony Rothman, et al. For the intelligent layman. Subjects include: cosmological models of the universe; black holes; the neutrino; the search for extraterrestrial intelligence. Introduction. 46 black-and-white illustrations. 192pp. 5⅜ × 8½. 24587-X Pa. $6.95

THE FRIENDLY STARS, Martha Evans Martin & Donald Howard Menzel. Classic text marshalls the stars together in an engaging, non-technical survey, presenting them as sources of beauty in night sky. 23 illustrations. Foreword. 2 star charts. Index. 147pp. 5⅜ × 8½. 21099-5 Pa. $3.50

FADS AND FALLACIES IN THE NAME OF SCIENCE, Martin Gardner. Fair, witty appraisal of cranks, quacks, and quackeries of science and pseudoscience: hollow earth, Velikovsky, orgone energy, Dianetics, flying saucers, Bridey Murphy, food and medical fads, etc. Revised, expanded In the Name of Science. "A very able and even-tempered presentation."—The New Yorker. 363pp. 5⅜ × 8. 20394-8 Pa. $5.95

ANCIENT EGYPT: ITS CULTURE AND HISTORY, J. E Manchip White. From pre-dynastics through Ptolemies: society, history, political structure, religion, daily life, literature, cultural heritage. 48 plates. 217pp. 5⅜ × 8½. 22548-8 Pa. $4.95

SIR HARRY HOTSPUR OF HUMBLETHWAITE, Anthony Trollope. Incisive, unconventional psychological study of a conflict between a wealthy baronet, his idealistic daughter, and their scapegrace cousin. The 1870 novel in its first inexpensive edition in years. 250pp. 5⅜ × 8½.   24953-0 Pa. $4.95

LASERS AND HOLOGRAPHY, Winston E. Kock. Sound introduction to burgeoning field, expanded (1981) for second edition. Wave patterns, coherence, lasers, diffraction, zone plates, properties of holograms, recent advances. 84 illustrations. 160pp. 5⅜ × 8¼. (Except in United Kingdom)   24041-X Pa. $3.50

INTRODUCTION TO ARTIFICIAL INTELLIGENCE: SECOND, EN-LARGED EDITION, Philip C. Jackson, Jr. Comprehensive survey of artificial intelligence—the study of how machines (computers) can be made to act intelli-gently. Includes introductory and advanced material. Extensive notes updating the main text. 132 black-and-white illustrations. 512pp. 5⅜ × 8½.   24864-X Pa. $8.95

HISTORY OF INDIAN AND INDONESIAN ART, Ananda K. Coomaraswamy. Over 400 illustrations illuminate classic study of Indian art from earliest Harappa finds to early 20th century. Provides philosophical, religious and social insights. 304pp. 6⅜ × 9⅜.   25005-9 Pa. $8.95

THE GOLEM, Gustav Meyrink. Most famous supernatural novel in modern European literature, set in Ghetto of Old Prague around 1890. Compelling story of mystical experiences, strange transformations, profound terror. 13 black-and-white illustrations. 224pp. 5⅜ × 8½. (Available in U.S. only)   25025-3 Pa. $5.95

ARMADALE, Wilkie Collins. Third great mystery novel by the author of *The Woman in White* and *The Moonstone*. Original magazine version with 40 illustrations. 597pp. 5⅜ × 8½.   23429-0 Pa. $7.95

PICTORIAL ENCYCLOPEDIA OF HISTORIC ARCHITECTURAL PLANS, DETAILS AND ELEMENTS: With 1,880 Line Drawings of Arches, Domes, Doorways, Facades, Gables, Windows, etc., John Theodore Haneman. Sourcebook of inspiration for architects, designers, others. Bibliography. Captions. 141pp. 9 × 12.   24605-1 Pa. $6.95

BENCHLEY LOST AND FOUND, Robert Benchley. Finest humor from early 30's, about pet peeves, child psychologists, post office and others. Mostly unavailable elsewhere. 73 illustrations by Peter Arno and others. 183pp. 5⅜ × 8½.
                                                    22410-4 Pa. $3.95

ERTÉ GRAPHICS, Erté. Collection of striking color graphics: *Seasons, Alphabet, Numerals, Aces* and *Precious Stones*. 50 plates, including 4 on covers. 48pp. 9⅜ × 12¼.   23580-7 Pa. $6.95

THE JOURNAL OF HENRY D. THOREAU, edited by Bradford Torrey, F. H. Allen. Complete reprinting of 14 volumes, 1837–61, over two million words; the sourcebooks for *Walden*, etc. Definitive. All original sketches, plus 75 photographs. 1,804pp. 8½ × 12¼.   20312-3, 20313-1 Cloth., Two-vol. set $80.00

CASTLES: THEIR CONSTRUCTION AND HISTORY, Sidney Toy. Traces castle development from ancient roots. Nearly 200 photographs and drawings illustrate moats, keeps, baileys, many other features. Caernarvon, Dover Castles, Hadrian's Wall, Tower of London, dozens more. 256pp. 5⅜ × 8¼.
                                                    24898-4 Pa. $5.95

AMERICAN CLIPPER SHIPS: 1833–1858, Octavius T. Howe & Frederick C. Matthews. Fully-illustrated, encyclopedic review of 352 clipper ships from the period of America's greatest maritime supremacy. Introduction. 109 halftones. 5 black-and-white line illustrations. Index. Total of 928pp. 5⅜ × 8½.
25115-2, 25116-0 Pa., Two-vol. set $17.90

TOWARDS A NEW ARCHITECTURE, Le Corbusier. Pioneering manifesto by great architect, near legendary founder of "International School." Technical and aesthetic theories, views on industry, economics, relation of form to function, "mass-production spirit," much more. Profusely illustrated. Unabridged translation of 13th French edition. Introduction by Frederick Etchells. 320pp. 6⅛ × 9¼. (Available in U.S. only)
25023-7 Pa. $8.95

THE BOOK OF KELLS, edited by Blanche Cirker. Inexpensive collection of 32 full-color, full-page plates from the greatest illuminated manuscript of the Middle Ages, painstakingly reproduced from rare facsimile edition. Publisher's Note. Captions. 32pp. 9⅜ × 12¼.
24345-1 Pa. $4.95

BEST SCIENCE FICTION STORIES OF H. G. WELLS, H. G. Wells. Full novel *The Invisible Man*, plus 17 short stories: "The Crystal Egg," "Aepyornis Island," "The Strange Orchid," etc. 303pp. 5⅜ × 8½. (Available in U.S. only)
21531-8 Pa. $4.95

AMERICAN SAILING SHIPS: Their Plans and History, Charles G. Davis. Photos, construction details of schooners, frigates, clippers, other sailcraft of 18th to early 20th centuries—plus entertaining discourse on design, rigging, nautical lore, much more. 137 black-and-white illustrations. 240pp. 6⅛ × 9¼.
24658-2 Pa. $5.95

ENTERTAINING MATHEMATICAL PUZZLES, Martin Gardner. Selection of author's favorite conundrums involving arithmetic, money, speed, etc., with lively commentary. Complete solutions. 112pp. 5⅜ × 8½.
25211-6 Pa. $2.95

THE WILL TO BELIEVE, HUMAN IMMORTALITY, William James. Two books bound together. Effect of irrational on logical, and arguments for human immortality. 402pp. 5⅜ × 8½.
20291-7 Pa. $7.50

THE HAUNTED MONASTERY and THE CHINESE MAZE MURDERS, Robert Van Gulik. 2 full novels by Van Gulik continue adventures of Judge Dee and his companions. An evil Taoist monastery, seemingly supernatural events; overgrown topiary maze that hides strange crimes. Set in 7th-century China. 27 illustrations. 328pp. 5⅜ × 8½.
23502-5 Pa. $5.95

CELEBRATED CASES OF JUDGE DEE (DEE GOONG AN), translated by Robert Van Gulik. Authentic 18th-century Chinese detective novel; Dee and associates solve three interlocked cases. Led to Van Gulik's own stories with same characters. Extensive introduction. 9 illustrations. 237pp. 5⅜ × 8½.
23337-5 Pa. $4.95